Total Transformation

Seven Sacred Steps to Freedom

ELIZABETH FLINT

BALBOA.
PRESS
A DIVISION OF HAY HOUSE

Balboa Press books may be ordered through booksellers or by contacting:

Balboa Press
A Division of Hay House
1663 Liberty Drive
Bloomington, IN 47403
www.balboapress.com
1 (877) 407-4847

Print information available on the last page.

ISBN: 978-1-9822-1131-8 (sc)
ISBN: 978-1-9822-1129-5 (hc)
ISBN: 978-1-9822-1130-1 (e)

Library of Congress Control Number: 2018910412

Balboa Press rev. date: 11/09/2018

This book is dedicated to my five gurus: Mom,
Dad, Nick, Griffin and Cassidy.
Thank you for believing in me and teaching me every single day
how to show up as my best self.

Acknowledgments

Writing a book is like having a baby. The beginning is rough and scary. You feel something unfamiliar growing within you and you know it's eventually going to want to come out. The middle is bliss. You feel good, powerful, energized. Towards the end you do a lot of worrying and rearranging of things in preparation. And during the last bit, just before the baby or the book is born, you feel swollen, irritable and completely terrified, but at the same time you're more than ready for what's been growing inside of you to come out. And when it does, in that moment when it passes from inside of you to outside of you, it is no longer yours and yours alone. You then have to share it with the rest of the world.

I want to acknowledge with deep gratitude the women who were my midwives and doulas in the process of giving birth to this book: my life and writing mentor, Alida Brill, my coach, editor and friend, Toni Robino, and my advocate, champion and publishing partner, Lisa Weinert. I would also like to acknowledge my amazing husband, who held my hand while I cried and pushed, and my friend Rich Horowitz, who believed in me enough to contribute to this project.

With all that I am, I thank you all.

Contents

Introduction

The Caterpillar and the Butterfly

While reading *The Very Hungry Caterpillar* to my son, I was struck by how well this simple story portrays the journey many of us must take. We start out hungry, looking everywhere for something to fill us up. We try a bit of this, a nibble of that, a heaping serving of something else, but we're still hungry. Some of us go along like this for many years, tricking ourselves into believing the next sweet treat, the next promise of a quick fix, will be the one that finally satiates the hunger, that deep longing within us.

Buddhists call this the suffering of the Hungry Ghosts. These hungry ghosts are beings with huge mouths and bellies, yet their throats are as skinny as needles. Though they can never get enough from the outside to nourish the hunger within, they keep trying, which keeps them trapped in the prison of their own wanting.

The hungry caterpillar, however, in its furry, sluggish wisdom, eventually realizes that all this grasping and overindulgence leads not to satisfaction but to a really bad tummy ache. On the seventh day, the day of rest and renewal, the caterpillar eats just one green leaf and feels much better.

Then she knows, as nature tells her, that it's time to go inward. She wraps herself up in a cocoon. The children's book doesn't mention what the caterpillar goes through to become a butterfly, though. Inside the cocoon, the caterpillar completely liquefies. At one point, all that remains is her DNA, which instructs that liquidated self to turn from a furry little worm into a magnificent butterfly. Once this transformation is complete, the butterfly emerges from its cocoon in all its brilliance for the outside world to enjoy. My son loves when I make the last two cardboard pages of the book into wings so the butterfly can fly away.

As humans, we can learn so much from this creature. We come into the world as hungry little caterpillars, hungry for love and ravenous for experience. Around our teen years, most of us begin to sense that something isn't quite right. Our bodies are changing, our thoughts and ideas are changing; we're starving for purpose and fulfillment. Most of us are not given the opportunity or permission to crawl into a chrysalis in order to liquefy all our past wanting into the most basic essence of who we are. We aren't given the time and space to fall apart so that we may come together again in a new way and emerge embodying the magnificence that is our destiny.

In some cultures, such as the native cultures of the Americas, young people have traditionally been given this opportunity in the form of a vision quest, sent out into the wild with no food or water in order to strip away everything that is not essential, to reclaim their eternally satiated selves and to emerge as adults, not just physically but spiritually, mentally and emotionally as well, so that they may claim their rightful place in the world.

When I first read about vision quests in high school, I told my mother I needed to go on one. "You are not going into the woods by yourself," she replied. "Are you crazy or do you just want an excuse to do drugs?" I understand why she responded like this. It wasn't something people did. It certainly wasn't something she had ever done. But funny enough, my father, an avid hunter, spent several weeks a year out in the woods sitting quietly by himself, tracking deer, caribou and elk. Although I'm a vegetarian and would have a very hard time killing an animal, I understood his need to go deep into nature, to leave behind all the comforts and distractions of life and reconnect to his primal self.

Was I crazy, as my mother had asked? At the time and for many years after, I thought I might be. Nonetheless, after college graduation I chose to embark on a five year vision quest of my own creation, which took me from India to California, to Australia, back to my hometown of St. Louis, Colorado and eventually to New York, where I've stayed.

It was less about the locations I traveled to and more about the places within myself, places that took me from my perpetual ghostly hunger to a state of being in which I recognize and inhabit my magnificence much of the time.

Through yoga and meditation I learned how to inhabit my body and stop letting my thoughts control me. Through Body/Mind Reconditioning, I developed the ability to see things from a new perspective, to change old habits and create new ones that serve me better. Through shamanism, I tapped into the wellspring of energy present in the unseen world and learned how to use it to heal myself and others.

This journey is not for the faint of heart. It's not for those who want to stay safe in what they already know. It's for those who understand the essence of these words from the poem "Risk," by Elizabeth Appell's (formerly Lassie Benton): "The day came when the risk to remain tight in the bud became more painful than the risk it took to blossom."[1] It's for those prepared to be liquefied by the universe in order to touch the deepest ground of their being and emerge into magnificent flight.

Total Transformation is a vision quest for the hungry ghost in all of us. It's a chrysalis for the caterpillar seeking to let go of the suffering of physical illness, mental stress and strife, emotional hardship and spiritual confusion. This book will help you to break out of your cocoon in order to live in communion with your true essence—the beauty the universe has intended for you—and lead a life of abundance, health, joy, equanimity and trust.

Risking Happiness

Many people would rather stay safe in what they already know, even if it's painful, than risk stepping into the unknown. On my journey, I've learned that if we don't accept the opportunities for growth that life offers, life will find a way to *make* us grow, and the growth we resist is often much more painful than the growth we embrace. Just like the

[1] John F Kennedy University adult education brochure, Orinda, CA, 1979

hungry caterpillar, we can go on for only so long gobbling up the quick fixes and the temporary pleasure before we get a tummy ache and say, "Enough. I give up. I'm ready to see what else is out there."

One of my friends spent more than twenty years running from his addiction to alcohol. He covered it up well and excelled at work, but his relationships fell apart and his body suffered. Not until the pain he felt from doing things the way he had always done them became so severe did he surrender to the possibility that there was a better way. He started to think it might be better to deal with the pain he'd been trying to manage with alcohol than to let the alcoholism consume him. So he went into rehab, but it took him several tries before he finally began to understand that no amount of drugs or alcohol can truly make our pain go away. Healing happens from the inside out. And while it initially takes more effort, in the long run it's so much easier to deal with our pain head-on and infinitely more fulfilling than turning to drugs or alcohol for a quick and fleeting fix.

In the process of healing, his life did fall apart. His marriage ended and he had to let go of most of the friends he had clung to since high school, as they weren't supporting his transformation. But he emerged from the process as someone I admire. I can trust him now. Our relationship is deeper than it has ever been because *he's* deeper than he's ever been. Not everyone would see his story as having a happy ending, given the fact that he lost so much, but I do. Actually, I see it as a happy beginning. Like the caterpillar turning into the butterfly, he's a completely different person from who he once was, one with the potential to live a life of true significance and purpose.

Maybe your issues aren't life-or-death. Maybe you're feeling it's time to make a career change but you're frightened of taking that leap and not sure where to leap to. Maybe you need to take better care of your body but you feel overwhelmed by all the options out there and you need some support to shift your habits. Perhaps everything is going great in your career but you can't seem to find a partner to share your life. The practices in this book can help you let go of what's preventing you from experiencing all the abundance life has to offer.

Wheels That Heal

The path of Total Transformation is based on the chakras, a complex system of energy centers within our beings that relate to our physical and emotional bodies as well as our minds and spirits. The word *chakra* means "wheel" in Sanskrit. There are seven main chakras, or wheels of energy, in the body: at the base of the spine, the center of the pelvis, the solar plexus, the heart, the throat, the brow center and the crown. Chakras aren't organs we could find inside a human body if we performed a dissection; they're more like the electrical currents that run through wires than the wires themselves. We can't see them any more than we can see air, sound or God, but we can see evidence of their existence everywhere.

When the chakras are functioning optimally, they're like turbines turning wind into usable energy. The chakras take the vital life force that's all around us and funnel it into the places it needs to go to help us with everything from daily bodily functions to the experience of transcending space and time. Like our physical organs, when the chakras are blocked or under stress they don't function as well as they should. Whereas you might do a cleanse to detoxify your liver, a cleansing breath practice or a visualization may help clear a particular chakra. In my shamanic training, we learned how to clear chakras using a stone. This method is very effective and something you can explore with a qualified practitioner, but there are also subtler methods we'll explore in this book that you can do on your own.

The chakra system came about in India before the time of the Buddha and Christ, as part of an experimental process done by yogis who had broken with the religious dogma of the time to seek a direct experience of knowing God through their own physical bodies and minds. They found that in deep states of meditation, they could perceive certain areas of the body that held strong centralized energy, and they had extrasensory experiences of those energy centers, which gave off specific colors, sounds and sensations. Then through the development of Tantra yoga, they related sacred images to these energy centers. Ancient yogis meditated on these centers as a way to transcend the physical body and unite with the divine. As time passed, yogis and other mystics began to see the chakras as energetic organs that, when functioning optimally, balanced the physical, emotional, mental and spiritual aspects of our being. Shamans of the Americas have used the chakra system for thousands of years as a tool to indicate, diagnose and remedy wounds in the energy body believed to be left from past-life, ancestral or present-life experiences

I've found that we're best-served if we think of the chakras both as energetic organs and as metaphors for the several stages of our personal transformation. We can use the symbology of the chakras to aid us in working with each one of these stages.

Each of the seven traditional chakras offers lessons, work and the possibility of deep transformation. (There are nine in the shamanic tradition, two of them located outside the physical body.) Although we can't directly measure the effects of working with the chakras, I've experienced them for myself and watched countless others, even people who didn't subscribe to the energetic theory, experience profoundly transformative effects.

The Tools of Total Transformation

Total Transformation is a culmination of nearly two decades of exploration, experimentation and fine-tuning. Through working with thousands of students and clients, I've developed an approach to healing and transformation that creates lasting change. This is not a one-size-fits-all approach. It's a compilation of wisdom, yoga practices, meditations, Body/Mind Reconditioning techniques and shamanic healing principles designed to serve those who are ready to take control of their lives.

Four-Pronged Approach

1. Yoga postures to stimulate the physical body parts related to each chakra
2. Meditation to clear the mind and harness our mental energy
3. Body/Mind Reconditioning to change our habits on a subconscious and conscious level
4. Powerful questioning to shift our thinking and open us up to new possibilities

This four-pronged approach to transformation addresses the conscious mind as it relates to each chakra and incorporates shamanic healing to heal the energy centers themselves. The process is intended to remove blockages and heal wounds that keep these energy centers and their related physical and mental formations from functioning properly so that they may then become power hubs along the central channel of the spine. This allows us to integrate and transcend the limitations we've lived with so that we can step into the freedom that's possible for all of us.

Yoga

Yoga has become a mainstream activity in our culture. In Manhattan alone there are more than three hundred yoga studios and hundreds of thousands of practitioners. When people ask me what kind of yoga I teach, I answer, "Whatever kind my students need." One of my private clients who has a hip replacement and is recovering from a serious illness had attended a group session in which the teacher used loud music and taught a very vigorous form of Vinyasa flow yoga. Afterward, when my client mentioned that she does private lessons, the teacher responded that private yoga is therapeutic and therefore not "real" yoga. I have to say I was really disappointed to hear this. In my opinion, real yoga is any yoga you practice with your full attention and intention. Real yoga, according to the Yoga Sutras, has very little to do with the physical practice. Real yoga is a practice of quieting the mind. I encourage you as you approach the yoga postures in this book to give them your full attention and intention. I would rather you lie on your back in Savasana (Corpse Pose or Final Relaxation) than force your body to do something that's out of alignment with what you need.

The yoga postures in this book are placed in specific chapters to assist you in the work of those chapters. For example, in Chapter 2 as we work on healing the first chakra by grounding and honoring the past, we practice Vrksasana (Tree Pose) which helps us connect to our roots and begin to develop inner stability. The poses included are fairly simple but should be approached with care, especially if you're recovering from injury or illness.

One of my regular yoga students approached me after having been away for a few months recovering from an injury. "I tried other things to feel better," he said, "other ways of moving my body, but I don't know—something about the breathing and paying such close attention. There's nothing else like yoga."

"Yes!" I said. He understood the thing that first drew me to yoga and made me want to dedicate my life to it. Even if one never learns about the deeper philosophy of yoga, the benefits come from doing the practice. When Ashtanga yoga guru Patthabhi Jois said, "Practice, practice and all is coming," he meant that we can study and philosophize all we want, but until we get on the mat to move our bodies, deepen our breath and pay very close attention, we will not receive the benefits of yoga.

Meditation

Meditation is also becoming increasingly popular in mainstream culture. You can attend classes, download apps, pay thousands of dollars for secret mantras or go on a ten-day silent retreat. Any one of these things may help you develop a meditation practice, but essentially meditation, like yoga, is simply a practice of quieting the mind. When you train your mind to focus on one thing at a time, whether it's a mantra or a guided visualization or the breath, the mind releases its distractions and becomes more spacious and relaxed. This leads us to a deeper sense of well-being in all areas of life.

There are as many styles and approaches to meditation as there are teachers. Over the years, I've tried many of those methods and studied with numerous teachers to discover that what's most important isn't the style of meditation we do but that we practice consistently and with enthusiasm. When we give ourselves fully to it, we receive the fruits of the practice.

During my own yoga teacher training in Australia, we began a ninety-minute meditation session at 6 a.m. every day. Some days it was torture. Some days it was bliss. I remember very clearly one morning when our teacher stopped the practice. "Greg, wake up!" she said. "You've been sleeping through meditation for six months. Not only is your neck getting shorter on the left side, but you're not gaining anything from being here."

I was glad she didn't choose me to chastise that day. I was very good at sitting still and very bad at staying present. I used most of those mornings as time to plan for the future, rewrite the past and jump from one random thought to the next. Not until our teacher yelled at Greg did I actually start trying to bring my awareness to the present moment. For some people, this is a natural thing to do. For me, it was as natural as riding a unicycle. But I kept trying, again and again and again, until eventually it started to work. My mind started to quiet down and I finally understood why we were sitting still with our eyes closed every morning. We were learning how to empty out everything that wasn't serving us. We were learning how to savor the sweetness of the present moment. We were learning how not to leave ourselves.

The guided meditations in this book correlate to the work set forth in each chapter. For example, in Chapter 3, as we work with pleasure and pain, we'll explore eating meditation. Mindful eating helps us observe our attachment to pleasure and our aversion to pain. When we're able to bring conscious awareness to both pleasure and pain, we come out of the shadows and into the light.

For complete yoga sequences and meditations, please refer to my audio recordings at **www.e-yoga.com/audio-yoga**.

Body/Mind Reconditioning

Body/Mind Reconditioning is a synthesis of techniques I've learned through training in neurolinguistic programming, the Sedona Method and transformational coaching.

During workshops and retreats, I include Body/Mind Reconditioning exercises to enhance the transformation process. While yoga and meditation are excellent tools for strengthening the body and quieting the mind, we all have pesky habits and hang-ups that can require more precise methods to release them from our lives. These include journaling prompts, reframing exercises, self-hypnosis, kinesthetic actions and visualization to break the patterns that cause us to repeat the same self-sabotaging actions again and again. In Chapter 4, when we work with turning fear into courage, you will be given a specific reframing exercise to release fear and cultivate your personal power so that you can step into new situations with strength and confidence.

Body/Mind Reconditioning will aid you in releasing patterns of stress, fear, anger and addiction that no longer serve you so that you can replace them with relaxation, fearlessness, peace and contentment. These practices include visualizations, purposeful questioning and physical techniques for bypassing the thinking mind and rewiring the nervous system so you can access your best self. In Chapter 4, when you work on turning your fear into courage, you will do a Body/Mind Reconditioning exercise to release the chronic state of fear directed at one situation we call a phobia. This phobia release technique helps us deflate that fear and replace the images of trauma in our minds with peaceful, relaxed images that serve our natural well-being.

Shamanic Healing

When people use the term *New Age* to describe shamanic healing, they couldn't be further off the mark. Shamanism has been part of many cultures for tens of thousands of years. Before modern medical techniques were developed, villages relied solely on the medicine man or woman to provide healing. Most of what shamanic healers do is restore balance, whether to the physical body, the mind or the community.

The founder of the Four Winds Society, Alberto Villoldo, tells many stories of the Peruvian shamans for whom these practices have been a way of life for many generations. In one story, he tells of a medicine woman who comes to a village that's suffering a great drought. The villagers beg her to perform a ceremony or a rain dance and are disappointed when, instead, she goes to the edge of the village, meditates and fasts for three days. When she returns, she brings the rain with her. She tells the villagers that she didn't make it rain—rather, she brought herself into full alignment with the rain and it came. Through shamanic healing, we can bring ourselves into full alignment with health, happiness, prosperity and wisdom.

Shamanism is an extensive body of wisdom practices developed over thousands of years in many parts of the world. The basic unifying principle of shamanism is that we as humans are meant to live in harmony with our surroundings, both natural and supernatural. Shamans believe that only a thin veil separates our everyday awareness from the awareness of the energetic realm. They also generally believe that when we are in right relationship with the earth, the sky, the plants, the animals and the spirits, we experience life as it is meant to be. Much of the work needed on our planet is the work of coming into right relationship with our environment and with one another.

The shamanic offerings in this book are based on the healing practices of the Laika people of Peru and the training I received through the Four Winds Society. The most valuable wisdom I've gained from these practices is that when we're in alignment within ourselves, the world around us begins to reflect that and our true purpose is revealed. These practices will help you clear out dense energy from your system and reclaim the parts of your being that have been out of alignment.

If shamanic healing is something that calls you, please visit www.thefourwinds.com for more information on how to become an energy-medicine health coach.

Working with This Book

Whenever I open a new book that promises to help me do anything better, whether it's cooking, parenting or developing my Jedi mind tricks, I'm eager to gobble up the information as quickly as possible. But I've found that like the caterpillar, I end up too full, unable to comprehend, digest or apply the information. When I suggested to a friend that he read one of my favorite spiritual books, Stephen Levine's *A Gradual Awakening*, he said he was surprised at how long it was taking him to get through it. He could only read a few pages at a time. Then he'd think about what the pages said, try to notice how the contents of the book were showing up in his life and try to integrate what he learned. This friend is a very patient person. I am not. I prefer to read a book straight through and then go back and do the exercises. Once I know where I'm going, I can sit back and enjoy the ride.

I suggest you use whatever approach works best for you. Do what you need to do in order to get the most benefit from what's on offer here. Take it slow and let it sink in or take it fast and read it as many times as you need to in order to receive the teachings. I often read or listen to the same audio book over and over for many months until I feel that I've assimilated the contents and I can then use what works for me and leave the rest behind.

The techniques in this book are simple and selective, based on the thematic work of each chapter. You can do them as many times as you want to or need to in order to receive the benefits. I will say that doing them once is not enough. That would be like running a single 5K and expecting to stay in shape for the rest of your life. This work is something you do a little of every day. The Yoga Sutras say transformation comes from a steady practice over a long period of time. How long? That's up to you. You'll know when to keep trying something and when it's time to let it go.

In this book I offer you my own insights and discoveries as well as my interpretation of the wisdom of the many teachers who have inspired and supported me on my journey. Here are just a few of my most wonderful teachers, whom you can also study with to deepen any aspect of this work: Matthew Sweeney, Rose Baudin, Sarah and Ty Powers, Ram Dass, Geneen Roth, Alberto Villoldo, Bill Damon, Sheryl Netzky, Stephen Feeley, Steven Levine, Stephen Cope, Thích Nhat Hanh, Pema Chodron and Tara Brach. I would also like to acknowledge my first and most influential teachers: my mother and father, without whom I never would have started on this path or believed that I had the capacity to share it with others.

Enjoy the journey.

CHAPTER 1

Happiness Is Possible

"It is not easy to find happiness in ourselves, and it is not possible to find it anywhere else."
— **Agnes Repplier, American essayist**

One day a man with tattoos and a motorcycle helmet walked into my yoga studio for the first time. He had practiced martial arts in the past, so the movements felt familiar to him in some ways, but the experience was much different. He felt as if, for the first time in his life, he was letting go rather than fighting.

He became a regular student at my studio. With very small morning classes, it was often just the two of us. During these private sessions, I learned that he was a police officer and that he had been on the force for only a few months when he was thrown into the wreckage of 9/11 to help with the rescue effort. It took several years for him to realize that he was struggling with PTSD as a result of that horrific day. He said that he and his fellow officers didn't talk about what had happened. They just went to the bar to forget about it. But something about yoga soothed him. It was just the right amount of effort and surrender. At the end of class, he could finally relax and let go.

A few years passed. The studio closed. He left the police force and moved away in search of the lost parts of himself. In California, he took a yoga teacher-training course, and when he came back to New York he decided to pursue yoga as a career. He became one of my first apprentices in the advanced teacher training. He also worked at the yoga studio where I started teaching after my own studio closed. There he met a woman at the front desk who rocked his world. They became inseparable and were soon engaged.

A few years later I had the great honor of marrying them. And my three-year-old son had the honor of sticking his fingers into their four-tier fondant cake before any of the guests had a chance to see it. Thank God the pastry chef was on duty and had time to smooth it out before the reception! Of course, the bride had seen this from her dressing room window, and when she didn't freak out, I knew she was good people and more of a yogi than I was.

After the wedding, life got busy for all of us. A year or so passed and I didn't hear from him. Then one day I saw him at a teachers' meeting. Afterwards, over tea, he said he'd been going through a rough time. He and his wife had been separated for a few months. Through therapy, he realized that he'd never really dealt with the pain he carried around about his father, who had been an abusive alcoholic and wasn't really in the picture when he was growing up.

He knew that in order to let go of that pain, he'd have to forgive his father, so he traveled to the other side of the world to meet him and forgive him. Not because what his father had done was okay but because holding on to the pain of it was causing him to suffer as much as his father and he was ready to be free.

Once he let go of the huge burden of resentment toward his father, he was able to heal and move forward. A few months after our talk, he announced that he would become a father to his own daughter. I'm certain he'll be an incredible father, not just because he's kind and loving but also because he knows what it's like to live in suffering and fear and he knows that in order to live in freedom and joy, we have to face ourselves, we have to face our problems, we have to forgive and we have to let go.

Not only did he change his whole life, but now as a yoga teacher he also changes the lives of many other people on a daily basis. This is the process of Total Transformation. This is the process of living a conscious life. This way of living isn't always easy, but it's always worth the effort. Over the course of almost twenty years, I've watched so many people, including myself, transform their lives through the practices in this book. I encourage you to open up to the possibility, whether you think you're broken beyond repair or you think your life is great and you don't need any help, that greater freedom and peace are always available to you. It is possible for everyone who chooses to pursue it, including you. You just have to open up, step in and let go.

"If it were not possible for you to be free from suffering, I would not teach you how." — **The Buddha**

The Buddha said, "Life is suffering." That doesn't seem like a very uplifting way for a spiritual teacher to begin his teachings, but upon close investigation, we discover that he was right. The suffering the Buddha refers to doesn't have to mean that someone is pulling our fingernails out with pliers or that we're dying of a terribly painful disease. It's simply the state of wanting things to be different from how they are. Sometimes it's very pronounced, like when we finally have a blow-up with a partner and all the rage comes out in words or physical violence. But most of the time it manifests more subtly, as that mental list of things we should be doing but don't have time for. It's the running commentary about all the stupid things we say when interacting with others. It manifests as negative energy toward people who appear to be different from us. However it appears, we all have it, and unless we're pursuing a consciousness, the suffering is most often simply being ignored or numbed by distractions, addictions and projection—as in, we project onto others the things that bother us about ourselves.

Though the Buddha said that life is suffering, he also promised that there's a way out, not once we get to heaven or in the next lifetime but in this lifetime. "If it were not possible for you to be free from suffering, I would not teach you how," he said. We can employ the many tools of mindful living to free ourselves from suffering.

Like with a caterpillar making the transition to a butterfly, the only real and lasting way out is through. The process involves shining a light on all the places we'd rather not look—the fear, the resentment, the guilt, the regrets—and turning these sources of suffering into sources of strength and wisdom that allow us to move through life with more equanimity and ease.

We Are Not What We Think

The Bible says our carnal nature, or flesh, is what causes us to suffer. The Buddha called it craving and aversion, and the Yoga Sutras call it delusion—believing that not only our happiness but also who we *are* is defined by what happens to us. If this were true, Jesus would have been absolutely miserable, Nelson Mandela wouldn't have lasted a year in prison and Mother Teresa would have thrown up her hands at the sight of India's impoverished, giving up before she even began. But she didn't.

All these iconic teachers persevered because they knew deep within themselves that this, too, would pass. Who we are is beyond anything that the world can throw at us. These teachers understood that the true cause of suffering isn't *out there*. It's in our own minds—identifying with the negativity of our thoughts. True freedom means freeing ourselves from that identification so we can connect to our divine eternal nature.

You're not there yet? Don't worry. You're not alone. The Yoga Sutras say that when the yogi's mind is still he can recognize his true and perfect nature, but at all other times he identifies with his thoughts, believing he *is* what he thinks. Therefore he suffers. Much of this suffering shows up in the form of attachment and aversion. When we're attached to something or someone, we don't want it to change and we don't want to lose it. Whether it's a delicious meal, a big event or a lover, everything that gives us pleasure will eventually change or end.

As a recovering food addict, I've observed this clearly through that perfect scoop of ice cream with hot fudge dripping down the sides, crushed hazelnuts and whipped cream on top. If I don't eat it because I want to save it, it will melt and I'll miss out on enjoying it. If I do eat it, it will eventually be gone and I'll mourn the loss. What to do? Eat it as quickly as possible and get another one. But then what? Another and another until the desire for pleasure that made us want the sundae has turned into a painful stomachache. Then we follow it up with guilt and self-loathing, punishing ourselves for being such gluttons. Eventually our stomachs shrink again, the slightest discomfort arises in our lives and the only thing we can think of to make us feel better is … a hot fudge sundae. This is the cycle of suffering, or samsara.

This doesn't mean we can't have a hot fudge sundae. It means that to truly enjoy it, we have to be able to also truly let it go. As the poet Mary Oliver writes in her poem "In Blackwater Woods," "To live in this world you must be able to do three things: to love what is mortal; to hold it against our bones knowing your own life depends on it; and, when the time comes to let it go, to let it go." Most of us have never learned the art of letting go—letting go of a great day, our youth or a loved one who's dying. It feels unnatural and wrong. But in reality, it's the perfection of life. Without letting go, we can't embrace the new. According to estimates from the Population Reference Bureau, as of 2015, 108.2 billion people have been born on this planet. Taking away the 7.4 billion people who were alive at that time, that means 100.8 billion people have died. If none of them ever died, we'd all be in serious trouble. A friend recently shared this riddle: "What's the leading cause of death?" The answer is, birth. Everyone, except maybe Edward Cullen and his family, dies. It's part of the experience of being human. When my best friend died of cystic fibrosis, I thought nothing would ever fill the void in my heart. But nine months later my first child was born, and my heart again overflowed with unconditional love.

Animals, plants, relationships and businesses die, too, each time making space in the world for something new to be born. If we don't let go of what needs to die, we can't receive what needs to be born.

Besides not letting go, aversion also causes us to suffer. How often do we build up in our minds a negative expectation about someone or something that completely clouds the reality of the situation? We have one bad experience with someone wearing a blue shirt and then every time we see someone in a blue shirt we get agitated. Some of us have never even seen someone in a blue shirt and we still want to obliterate those who wear them because someone we know told us how awful people in blue shirts are. "They're liars and cheaters who can't be trusted," that person said. Rather than spending time with someone in a blue shirt to find out for ourselves if this is true, we just adopt the opinions of those who have come before us. This is the energy that creates the various forms of hatred we grapple with in our society.

Aversion is useful in that it teaches us not to step out into traffic or put our hands on the hot stove, but most often it keeps us trapped in a bubble that gets smaller and smaller every time we indulge it. My friend's son is one of the pickiest eaters I've ever met. At some point he tried a vegetable and didn't like the taste, so he decided not to eat that vegetable. As he continued to indulge his aversion, his diet grew more and more homogenized until he would eat nothing but meat, bread and cheese. Granted, many combinations of these three foods are available, but he's missing out on all the vitamins, nutrients, flavors and textures of the other food groups based on a negative experience that happened many years ago. When we let aversion take over, we miss out on the actual experience of the moment. We don't allow things to be as they are. We experience them only as they were.

When I first moved to New York, I had a strong aversion to rats. When I'd see one waddling over the rails in the subway tunnel, I'd feel as if I were going to vomit. One day as I walked toward the stairs to leave the station, I felt something soft and furry scuttle over my sandaled foot. I leaped into the air like someone with ants in her pants and screamed out an "Ahh!!" Because it was New York, no one really noticed, but I realized that I'd let an eight-inch rodent completely terrify me. I didn't want to live in fear, so the next time I saw one of those little guys on the rails, I decided to just watch it, to breathe and stop myself from reacting. Soon I was reminded of a college friend who had a pet rat named Tootles. Tootles was cute and friendly. (Tootles had probably been vaccinated.) I tried to extend the same kindness to the subway rat that I had extended to Tootles (without touching it, of course), and I realized that it wasn't as scary as I thought. I could actually relax and let the rat go about his business. I didn't need to exterminate him to exterminate my fear.

Everything Is Impermanent Except ...

If attachment and aversion are the root causes of our suffering, how do we let these patterns go in order to experience true joy and peace? We have to recognize that everything in this world is impermanent and that we can't control anything outside ourselves. We must also come into alignment with what *is*.

If you've ever truly loved a pet, you've experienced the law of impermanence on a deep level. My dog Rosie came to me unexpectedly. I was sitting in the old Baptist church where I spent most of my Sunday mornings as a child, this time to celebrate my grandparents' fiftieth wedding anniversary. My aunt brought in a tiny black puppy with brown eyebrows and set it in my grandpa's lap. "No!" he said. "I don't want another dog." I took her from his lap into my arms and fell instantly and deeply in love. Over the course of twelve years, I watched her grow from a puppy to an old woman.

As a puppy, she followed so close to my left heel when we walked that I would turn and think I'd lost her. As she grew into a teenager, she would bolt out the front door whenever it opened and I'd spend twenty minutes trying to corral her back inside. Later in her life, when I opened the door to go for a walk, she looked up at me as if to say, "Well, if we must."

When she developed congestive heart failure, I grappled with the fear of losing her. I couldn't imagine my life without her. For over a year, I watched her every move, wondering when the moment that her heart would give out would come. Everyone told me that she'd let me know when she was ready to go. I tried to listen to her closely, but all I could hear most of the time was my own resistance and fear. We had the hospice vet come to our home three times to put her down, and each time we sent her away.

One day, Rosie and I were sitting on the back steps in the afternoon sun listening to the birds chirping. As the breeze rustled her fur, we looked into each other's eyes.

It's okay, I could feel her say. I didn't hear it. I just felt it.

Tears streamed down my face and my shoulders dropped. I knew she was ready to go.

We sent her off with shamanic prayers and peanut butter in the very spot on the living room floor where she'd spent most of her later days. I lay down next to her and watched her spirit leave her body. One moment it was in and the next it was out. I knew in that instant that she hadn't disappeared—she'd just moved on. All that fear I'd had about her death dissolved. We were both at peace.

The essence of who we both are has not changed from that first day in the church and will not change for eternity. It's the only thing that doesn't change. It's our divinity. To recognize this helped me to let go of how it was when she was a cute little puppy and a healthy dog and to embrace how it is now that she's not there to greet me at the door or lick the yogurt container. I can always close my eyes and see her looking back at me, so sweetly, with pure unconditional love.

You Are the Only One You Can Control

Shunryu Suzuki writes in his book *Zen Mind, Beginner's Mind*:

> Even though you try to put people under control, it is impossible. You cannot do it. The best way to control people is to encourage them to be mischievous. Then they will be in control in a wider sense. To give your sheep or cow a large spacious meadow is the way to control him. So it is with people: first let them do what they want, and watch them. To ignore them is not good. That is the worst policy. Just watch them, without trying to control them.

As a parent, it's tempting to try to control everything our children do. What they eat, when they sleep, how they behave in public. It all feels like a reflection of who we are as parents and people. We feel judged if our children misbehave in public. We worry they'll starve if they don't eat their dinner. We want them to sleep through the night so that we aren't exhausted at work the next day. Parenting is a dance of control and surrender, a dance you can't practice in advance. You can only learn the steps as you go.

At the age of three, my son started to cry every time he didn't get what he wanted. My responses ranged from just giving him what he wanted to make him feel better to trying to make him stop crying to make myself feel better. After a few months of this, I remembered Suzuki's quote and decided to just watch him go through his tantrum. I would sit with him, calm myself and watch the tears roll down his face, offering a gentle expression but no words. I could feel the agitation in my own body rise and then dissipate. After about five minutes, he would get sick of crying, usually forgetting what he was crying about, and move on to the next activity.

Through these tantrums I learned that it's not my fault and it's not my job to make him stop. My job is to hold space for him until he learns how to stop on his own. In doing this, we've both learned to cultivate a bit more equanimity from within. And so it is with our spouses, co-workers, parents, siblings and friends. It's not our job to stop them from behaving in a way we see as problematic. It's our job to hold space for them and to stop our own problematic behaviors.

We Must Align with What *IS* to Have What We Want

If this seems like a paradox, that's because it is. Most spiritual teachings are. Have you ever been stuck in traffic, running late for an appointment, and started to tense up? Your blood pressure increases. Your palms get sweaty. Your nervous system gears up for a fight. Except that that fight isn't going to happen anywhere but in your own mind. As a friend once joked, "The biggest problem with a traffic jam is all these other cars."

We think the problem is *out there*. It's the other cars on the road. If they weren't there, we could just drive and be on time. But the truth is that we're part of the traffic. We have just as much responsibility as everyone else on the road for making it too crowded. When you live in New Jersey and work in Manhattan, traffic is inevitable. The Holland Tunnel is like a drinking straw that a rushing river has to pass through. Often, the river doesn't flow. It creeps along like a slug, making everyone angry and anxious.

One afternoon I parked on the main road that leads into the tunnel. As I flipped on my turn signal and inched into the lane of slugs slurping along, the woman I'd inched out in front of started wailing on her horn. When I looked at her, she screamed something. She looked like a rabid animal. I'd never seen someone so upset and directing it toward me. It was like watching a movie character and knowing that I never again wanted to play that character in my own movie. Her behavior was so over-the-top that it stopped my mind from reacting. I realized that getting upset at her wouldn't have helped anyone. I just gestured for her to go in front of me and then sent her loving-kindness from behind, wondering how many moments I'd wasted by being furious over something I couldn't change. I still send gratitude to that woman because she cured my own road rage (or at least put it into remission). Now I can honestly say that most of the time, I no longer get upset when I'm driving. I can't say for sure that staying calm helps me get to work on time more often, but it sure seems that way, and on the less frequent occasion when I'm late, at least I arrive in a calm state, which is really what you want from your yoga and meditation teacher.

Thinking of that woman, the serenity prayer comes to mind. "God, give me the serenity to accept the things I cannot change, the courage to change the things I can and the wisdom to know the difference." When we're wise, we know we can't change the traffic or the way other people respond to it. But we *can* change our minds and the way we respond. In this wisdom, we do change our circumstances. We show up less often in scenes that provoke us and more often in ones that relax us because we're at ease in a wide range of experiences and we're tapped into the natural well-being of the universe.

Freedom from Suffering

If we think of suffering as something simple like a stomachache, then we can think of freedom from suffering as the absence of a stomachache. This may seem like no big prize unless you've ever had a terrible stomachache and then been free of it. Having experienced lower back pain for twenty years, I find that the absence of it is one of my greatest pleasures. A client of mine who suffers from chronic headaches would give anything for the simple absence of those headaches. Freedom from suffering frees up our physical, mental and emotional energy so we can begin to ask ourselves the question "What do I really want?"

Exercise:

Take a moment now to ask yourself this question: ***What do I really want?*** Close your eyes for a moment, allowing the answer to come. Then write it down.

Ask yourself again: ***What do I really want?*** Close your eyes again, allowing another answer to come, and then write it down. It may be the same answer or it may be different.

Do this five times. Then take a look at your answers.

What is at the heart of your answers?

For example, say you want a new job that challenges your skill set, allows you to earn more money and gives you more time to spend with your family. The essence of this want is the desire to grow, prosper, love and be loved.

If We Want to Be Happy

I've seen the Dalai Lama speak a few times, and I remember him saying, "Everyone just wants to be happy and be loved." Carl Jung asserted the five keys to happiness as good physical and mental health, good personal and intimate relationships, the ability to appreciate beauty in art and nature, a reasonable standard of living resulting from satisfying work and a philosophical or religious point of view that helps one cope with the "vicissitudes" of life. There are five elements that make up our human experience—the body, the mind, the heart, the soul and the spirit—and when we feed each aspect of ourselves, we're satiated. We're happy.

Often we think there's only one way to get what we want. For instance, for many years my husband thought the only way to feel a sense of purpose in his work was to become a successful filmmaker. While he's still working toward this dream, he's now able to recognize that his daily work, which he sometimes finds less exciting, affords him the time to play a crucial part in a theater company that feeds his artistic soul. Often what we seek is already available to us if we let go of needing it to be presented in a specific way.

In an article published 2014, *The Wall Street Journal* reported research showing that, overall, people with more money are more satisfied with their lives. However, above the income level of about $75,000 per household, people might be more satisfied but they don't experience positive emotions more often. The article said that experiences, though fleeting, bring us more happiness than things, and giving away money makes us happier than spending it on ourselves. The article concludes with this wisdom, "The bottom line: When you don't have much money, a little extra can go a long way, because you have more essential needs to fulfill. As you accumulate more wealth, however, it becomes more difficult to keep 'buying' more happiness."[i]

The story of the businessman and the fisherman illustrates this point. A Western businessman was at the pier of a small fishing village in Mexico when a fisherman docked a tiny boat. Inside the small boat were several large fish. The businessman was impressed by the fish and asked how long it had taken to catch them.

"Only a couple of hours," the fisherman replied.

The businessman asked why didn't he stay out longer and catch more fish.

"I have plenty for my family to eat today," the fisherman said.

Being that it was early afternoon, the businessman, used to working sixty to eighty hours a week, wondered what the fisherman did with the rest of his time.

"I play with my children, spend time with my wife, take siestas in the afternoon and spend time with my friends in the evening."

The businessman didn't say so, but he thought the fisherman was lazy and wasting his natural talent for fishing. He told the fisherman he could help him grow his business.

"If you spent more time fishing, you could buy a bigger boat and hire people to work for you. Then you could buy more boats and start your own company to sell your fish to the fisheries in big cities like where I'm from. You would make ten times as much money as you make now, but you would have to leave the village and move to one of the big cities to run your company."

The fisherman thought for a moment, "How long would this take?"

"About twenty years," the businessman said. "You wouldn't get to spend as much time with your children or your wife or your friends, but you could give them anything they want."

"Except time with me," he pointed out. "What would happen after twenty years?"

The businessman smiled. "You could sell your company for lots of money, move to a small fishing village and relax, spending time with your kids, your wife and your friends."

The fisherman thought for a moment and smiled. "I think I'll pass."

Often, our Western minds have a difficult time grasping the concept of "enough." We worship movie stars, athletes and business owners who, like Mark Zuckerberg, have so much more than enough that they often end up giving huge sums of it away. Having enough does help make us happy, but having more than enough does not help make us happier.

Subconsciously, we believe that if we have more than enough we'll be safe. We won't get hurt, we won't be lonely, we won't be scared. But the truth is, money, fame and success can't protect us from pain. It can only distract us for a while. The only way to develop true security in our lives is to let go of the belief that we can get it from outside and embrace the knowing that we must cultivate it on the inside.

We Can Have What We Really Want

This is the crux of Total Transformation—a process of deprogramming the mind and body in order to come into alignment with the natural well-being of the universe. When we try to get what we want from the outside in, we end up suffering more. When we turn inward and cultivate what we want from the inside out, our happiness becomes unwavering, our equanimity unshakable.

When I lived in a yoga ashram in my early twenties in San Francisco, there was a young woman who had lived there for more than five years. My newbie friend and I once asked her how long she planned to stay, to which she responded, "Until I become unshakable." She didn't say, "For another five years," or, "Until I'm ready to have a family." Her timeline came from a place deep within. Only she would know when she'd reached the most solid ground within herself and learned how to live from that place of being unshakable.

The process of Total Transformation is one path to becoming unshakable. Through the practices of yoga, meditation, Body/Mind Reconditioning and shamanic healing, we can clear out all the coping habits we've accumulated over the years that no longer work for us and replace them with ways of being in the world that support our highest good and serve the highest good of those around us.

Regardless of whether we cure every problem with our physical bodies, to learn how to become present in our bodies, to know our minds well and to see our hearts clearly is how we free ourselves from suffering. The Laika people of Peru believe that healing is different from curing. Curing means getting rid of a physical disease, while healing means clearing the imprints for that disease and transcending its cause, which may or may not show up as perfect physical health in this lifetime.

For many years, I measured my own success as a healer by whether my clients became "cured." I was elated if I was able to help them extinguish pain or release a destructive habit. Conversely, I felt defeated if they weren't rapidly cured. But after working with a client over the course of several years who struggled with chronic pain, I realized that the pain itself was the cure for many of the symptoms she'd been living with most of her life. The pain woke her up to her truth and forced her to surrender her ego. My job has been to hold space for her while she goes through that process. As I write this, my client still suffers from physical pain, but the depths to which she has traveled within herself, and the spiritual and emotional changes she has made as a result, are immeasurable.

Of course, we all want to feel good, and we deserve to experience the natural state of well-being that the universe provides. Once you've tasted that sweetness, there's no going back. Not really. Just like the moment I realized that I never wanted to practice road rage again. When I try it now, it feels forced and void of the charge it once held. When we asked our friend at the ashram how she would know when she had become unshakable, she said, "You just know, unequivocally."

"And then what?" I asked.

"Then you help other people do the same thing."

This is the work of the bodhisattva, the liberated being. As one of my teachers, Sarah Powers, says in her opening and closing prayer, "We are all suffering and awakening together." When we awaken to the way our lives have not been working and make the necessary changes that afford us a life of freedom, we are then free to help others do the same.

CHAPTER 2

Reclaiming Our Roots and Releasing Old Wounds

"People have a hard time letting go of their suffering. Out of a fear of the unknown, they prefer suffering that is familiar."

— Thích Nhất Hạnh, Buddhist Monk and Teacher

We usually think of forgiveness as something we give to those who have hurt us, something we do to make them feel better, to help them move past the guilt of whatever harm they caused us. In truth, forgiveness is something we do for ourselves. It's something we do to help us move past the pain of whatever it was that hurt us.

Forgiveness doesn't mean we approve of bad behavior, violence or betrayal. It simply means we would rather unburden ourselves of the weight of resentment or guilt than hold on to it, so that we can step into a lighter place of being.

Forgiveness is a conscious decision to let go, to stop punishing someone for a wrongdoing. It means we stop seeing that person as bad, evil or wrong. Forgiveness is especially important when we see ourselves that way. Whether we're forgiving another person or ourselves, we choose to forgive by starting to separate the action from the person. We start to see that the person made a decision that caused harm, but no matter how many harmful decisions that person has made, his or her essential nature is basic goodness. It can't be any other way. We can't take form here on Earth without having first come from the essential goodness of the universe that many call God. If we think we're bad or another person is inherently evil, we're calling the creator of the universe evil. And that's quite a demoralizing belief to carry around.

One of my teachers told a story about a woman whose teenage son was shot and killed by a gang member. I'm not sure if this story is truth or legend, but it holds a powerful lesson either way. The young gang member was convicted of murder and sentenced to prison time. Just as he was leaving the courtroom after his sentencing, the mother of the boy he killed stood up and said, "I'm going to kill you." Anyone could understand her rage, but at the time, no one actually understood what she meant, possibly not even her.

A few months later, she went to the prison to visit her son's killer. At first he didn't want to see her. Can you blame him, given what she'd said in the courtroom? Even with thick glass between them, he shook in fear of what she might say or do. But they just talked. She asked him about his life and family. She started to uncover the person behind the action. To his surprise, when she left, she asked him if he needed anything. He said no, not wanting to bother her.

After that first visit, she came back again and again, each time uncovering a little more about him, sharing a bit more about herself and her son. Several years later, when he was finally about to be released, she asked him what he would do when he got out. He had no idea. The gang was the only family he had. He had no money or skills and nowhere to live. The next time she visited, she surprised him with the news that she had arranged for him to start working at a local factory. Then she floored him by inviting him to come stay in her son's old bedroom. The old fear rose up inside him. How could this woman, the mother of the boy he shot, invite him into her home? *She must be planning her revenge*, he thought.

Still he agreed, and after several months of working in the factory and living in her home, she called him to the table to talk. *Here it comes*, he thought.

"Remember when I said in the courtroom that I was going to kill you?" she said.

His heart pounded as he nodded his head, remembering that horrible day.

"Well, I did," she said.

She went on to explain that rather than hating the boy who killed her son, she decided to pour all her hurt into transforming that boy from a killer into the kind of person she would have wanted her own son to be. At the end of her explanation, she paused. Then she asked if she could adopt him.

He was stunned. Having gone without any loving parents his whole life and knowing he had caused so much pain in her life, he couldn't fathom how she could possibly want to have him as her son.

"Are you sure?" he asked, quivering with emotion.

"I am sure. Just like you, I have no one to love," she said, choking back the tears. "We can love each other now. This is the only real justice that I can possibly imagine."

This is how we change people, not by persecution but by forgiveness and redemption.

Most of us will never be asked to forgive such a terrible act, but every one of us has been disappointed, violated, betrayed and hurt by someone. Just as each one of us has disappointed, violated, betrayed or hurt someone else. If we hold on to the pain, pain is what we will experience, not just once, as we did the first time, but again and again and again until it feels as if pain is the essence of who we are.

When the Romans captured Jesus and sentenced him to crucifixion, his most devoted disciple, Simon Peter, was given three chances to step up and declare his allegiance to and love for Christ, but each time he was too frightened. Each time someone asked, "Aren't you with him?" he said no. He denied the person he loved most out of fear for his own life. The Yoga Sutras say that even the wise cling to life out of fear of dying.

After Jesus was crucified and buried and rose from the dead, he appeared to Simon Peter from the shore while Peter was out fishing with his men. After the initial shock of seeing his beloved teacher again, fear set in. Peter had already decided that there was no way Jesus, living or not, would ever again trust him enough to use him for good. He had condemned himself as a traitor and a failure and decided he would never again be more than a fisherman. But Jesus had other plans for his most loyal disciple.

Simon Peter had denied Christ three times on the day he was taken to the cross. On this night, Jesus asked him in front of the other disciples and his fishing buddies, "Do you love me?"

"You know I do," Simon Peter replied.

Jesus asked him again, "Do you love me?"

"Yes." He said.

Jesus asked him a third time.

Again he replied, "Yes."

"Well then, take care of my sheep," Jesus said.

And in that moment it was clear to everyone that Jesus forgave him. He saw past the fearful decision that Peter had made and redeemed him. He made him the shepherd of his flock, the ones who believed he was the son of God and wanted to follow his teachings. He could have chosen one of the other disciples, one that hadn't denied knowing him. Just as that mother could have adopted any other boy if she just wanted to have someone to love. But like Jesus, she knew that redemption was the most powerful form of justice.

At its essence, forgiveness is love. When we forgive ourselves or someone else, we are choosing love above all else.

What Old Wounds Are You Holding On To?

A woman I know, although fiercely religious, has a habit of holding grudges. If someone says something she doesn't like or does something she thinks is wrong, she'll stop speaking to that person indefinitely. I used to wonder how she reconciled this with her Christian faith but have come to realize that the mind can justify almost anything to suit the way we perceive the world. That's why the Yoga Sutras advocate for learning to perceive our experience from a place of non-judgment, where rather than seeing what has happened as good or bad, we see it in terms of what we can learn. We use even the most difficult experiences as opportunities to gain wisdom and growth. From this vantage, rather than reacting to what has hurt us in a way that causes more pain, we can choose wisely how to best respond.

In the film *Eternal Sunshine of the Spotless Mind*, Kate Winslet's character agrees to a procedure that will erase her boyfriend, Jim Carrey's character, from her mind. This service is presented as a way of helping people let go of the pain of the past so they can move on. But if we completely forget about the painful experiences of our past, we don't learn or grow. Forgiveness means remembering the lessons and letting go of the pain that paralyzes us.

Think of a situation in your own life that has caused you pain, a person you resent or something you've done for which you haven't forgiven yourself. Write down this story that you've been telling yourself and others and read it aloud. Then write down the answers to the following questions:

- How does thinking about this story and telling this story make you feel?
- What images come into your mind?
- How do you feel in your body?
- What emotions arise as you recount this story?
- How does this story shape your perception of yourself, others and the world?
- What would it be like to let go of this pain? Not to erase the story from your memory, but to release the burden you've been carrying around?

Imagine the story you've been holding on to and the people you haven't forgiven. Imagine each person as someone just like you who wants to be loved and be happy. Acknowledge that the means they used to obtain love and happiness were harmful and that the harm may even have been intentional. Remember that the essence of each being is the same as that of all others, regardless of their actions. Note that when we're out of alignment with the universe, we suffer. Remember that those who inflict harm are suffering and that those who inflict the most harm suffer the most.

"Letting go gives us freedom, and freedom is the only condition for happiness. If, in our heart, we still cling to anything—anger, anxiety or possessions—we cannot be free." — Thích Nhất Hạnh, *The Heart of The Buddha's Teaching; Transforming Suffering into Peace, Joy and Liberation*

Forgiveness Meditation

This meditation will allow you to further release resentment and cultivate forgiveness. You can read through it and then do the meditation yourself or have someone else read it to you. The recorded version of this meditation and all others in this book are available at https://e-yoga. com/audio-yoga/.

Come to a seated position. Begin to breathe into your heart space. Notice the heart's natural capacity to expand and contract, expand and contract. This is what the physical heart does thousands of times a day without any interference. Just observe that expanding and contracting, expanding and contracting. *Pause.*

Think about your life from your very first memories and how your heart would expand with love at certain times and contract into itself at other times, how this natural capacity to feel your emotions helped you develop your sense of place in the world.

Inevitably, teachers, classmates, siblings and parents violated this natural expansion and contraction at times. We were forced to go beyond what felt natural for us, punished for something we didn't know was wrong, forced to spend time with someone we didn't want to open up to, made to feel somehow wrong or bad just for being ourselves. We may have strong memories or examples of how this happened or weak, vague ones, but we all have them. They're part of being human.

Take a moment to connect to the strongest, earliest memory or sense of having the natural capacity of your heart violated by someone else. If you can't think of anything, just imagine what that would have felt like or pick a more recent memory to work with.

See an image of yourself in that moment in your mind. Notice how you felt. Bow to who you were in that moment. Bow to the perfection that was present in you that was not being seen or honored. Now honor that version of you just as you were. In your mind's eye, tell that version of you that he or she is good, whole, worthy, that the natural experience of expansion and contraction is worthy of being honored. In your mind, you can sit with or hug or bow to this version of yourself. *Pause.*

Now bring your attention to the person or people who violated that sense of worthiness in you. Allow one person to come to the forefront. Staying connected to the natural capacity of your heart, look this person in the eye and see that they are just like you. They have a natural capacity to expand and contract that has been violated, and that's probably why they did the same to you. Offer this person your forgiveness. "I forgive you." Say it a few times and notice how it feels. "I forgive you for making me feel bad. I forgive you for hurting me. I forgive you for not honoring me." Say whatever feels most natural and true. *Pause.*

Then take that forgiveness a step further as a way of releasing the karma for both of you. Offer these words: "I honor who you are at your essence. At your essence you are whole and perfect, just like me."

Sit for a few moments with this person or group of people. If the desire to hug arises, you can do this in your mind. If the desire to keep your distance and simply bow arises, you can do this. If the desire is to remain silent and just be present, do this. Honor the way that you need to express your forgiveness. *Pause.*

Now come back to the present moment, come back to your own breath, to who you are right now. Honor yourself deeply in this moment. *Pause.*

Now remember a time when you violated the natural capacity of another person's heart, either by mistake or on purpose. Remember how you felt as you did this, how you felt afterward and how the person responded.

Go back to this time and place. First see the person you hurt and bow to him or her, acknowledging his or her inherent worthiness. Then say to this person, "I am deeply sorry for hurting you. I am sorry for violating your heart. Please forgive me." Imagine this person bowing to you as you did to those who hurt you, forgiving you for your mistake. *Pause.*

Now turn toward yourself, this version of you who caused pain to another. Bow to this version of yourself, honoring who you were in that moment. Acknowledge that even in causing pain to another, at your essence you are always whole and worthy. Say to yourself, "I forgive you for hurting another. I love you. I forgive you." You may want to hug this version of you or bow to it. Do whatever feels natural in the moment and be with that experience. *Pause.*

Now come back to your breath in this moment. Notice how the natural expansion and contraction of your heart may have changed or shifted. Honor the natural expanding and contracting. Honor who you are right now and who you have always been at your essence—whole, worthy and perfect. *Pause.*

Breathe. Come back to your body. Feel your body. Begin to notice the sounds around you. Begin to move your fingers and toes. Slowly open your eyes.

"If you let go a little you will have a little happiness. If you let go a lot you will have a lot of happiness. If you let go completely you will be free." – Achaan Chah, ***A Still Forest Pool: The Insight Meditation of Achaan Chah***

How Do We Truly Let Go?

A good friend once confided that a teacher had raped her in high school. While the experience was frightening and painful for her, she made a clear and conscious decision not to let it define who she was. She decided not to give her power to the man who had hurt her. Somewhere inside, she knew rape wasn't about sex but about the misguided belief that taking someone else's power makes us more powerful. She chose to continue seeing herself as a virgin until she later had sex with someone of her own choosing in a mutually respectful relationship. This isn't to say she didn't need support to heal. Through therapy, prayer and meditation, she was able to move on. At a certain point, she decided to let go of the fear and pain so she could live her life to the fullest.

Most of us would have a very difficult time doing what she did, especially at such a young age, but we all have the opportunity right now to let go of the wounds of the past that we've been holding on to and to recognize that nothing that's ever happened to us defines who we truly are.

When, however, we recognize ourselves getting caught up in the thought patterns that perpetuate our suffering, we can ask ourselves these simple questions:

- Do I want to suffer or do I want to be happy?
- Do I want to blame or do I want to love?

Asking these questions can get us "unstuck" so we can stop digging deeper into the hole of blame and suffering and climb up into the fresh air of our life in the present.

Fire of Transformation

At the end of many of my retreats, we build a fire. Each of us who has gone through the transformational process together finds a stick to represent something we want to let go of. We stand around the fire, holding space for one another. As the warm glow illuminates our faces, each person steps up and speaks aloud what they are releasing. He takes a moment to give thanks for that thing, even if it has been quite painful, and another moment to make the clearest intention possible to let it go. He throws the stick into the fire and watches it burn. This symbolizes the burning up of past karma. As the fire grows brighter from the offering of this stick, we're reminded that our inner light grows brighter each time we choose to let go.

Ultimately, as Ajahn Chah points out, we can't hold on to anything. All the things, all the people, all of the experiences of our lives are the river of life flowing through and around us. We all choose how we approach the river. We can stand in the middle and let the current swirl around us, we can bring buckets into the water and try to store up as much as possible or we can try our best to swim upstream. But eventually we all have to lie down and let the current take us and let the waters wash us clean of our grasping, clinging and fear.

Personal Fire Ceremony

Creating your own fire ceremony is a wonderful way to let go of what's no longer meant for you. If you can safely make a fire outside, that's a good way to go. But you can still create a ceremony if you live in an urban area. I often use a candle and toothpicks or some pieces of sage. Make your fire intentional. If you're in nature, choose the logs, sticks and twigs mindfully, as if you were letting them choose you.

Then sit for a moment before you light your fire. Call on the benevolent energy of the unseen world to support you in the act of letting go. Think about what you want to let go of. It can be one thing or a hundred things. And remember, letting go of something like our children doesn't mean we'll never see them again. It means that we can be more fully present with them, harboring less fear, worry and control.

When you're ready, light the fire. Watch the flame grow for a little while. Since fire has the energy to harm or to transform, shamans say to wait until the fire is "friendly" before approaching it. I like to make the fire friendly with a short prayer: "To the spirits of the Universe, to Mother Earth and to all the Wise Ancestors, thank you for your support and guidance, your sustenance and your love. Please hold space, bear witness and help me to truly let go of what needs to go and receive what I need to receive to be of the highest benefit to all beings."

In the Four Winds tradition, olive oil is offered to the fire three times. First to honor the four directions (south, west, north and east), second to honor the heavens and earth and third to honor all those who are present. When you do a fire ceremony alone, this obviously includes you. It also refers to those who are present energetically. Perhaps your best friend lives in another country or your favorite grandmother has passed away. Maybe there's a religious deity you'd like to invite. You can energetically invite them all to the fire through your prayers and intentions.

Once the fire feels friendly to you, choose the pieces of kindling one by one that represent the things you're letting go. Hold each one for a moment and say aloud what you're releasing. Throw it into the fire or drop it onto the candle flame. As you watch it burn down, draw the pure light of that flame back into you energetically. Do this for as many things as you choose.

When you finish, sit with the fire or the candle flame. Notice how you feel. Envision all the things you released being replaced with greater happiness and love. Thank the fire for its cleansing and its light. Cup your hands over the fire and bring that light toward your heart. Bow to the light within you and within the fire. Then blow out the candle or cover the flame. Close the space by expressing gratitude again to those who were present energetically. I like to repeat the opening prayer, adding more words of gratitude: "Thank you, spirits of the universe. Thank you, Mother Earth. Thank you, wise ancestors, for your support and guidance, your sustenance and your love. Thank you for holding space, bearing witness and helping me to truly let go of what needs to go. Thank you for helping me receive what I need to receive to be of the highest benefit to all beings."

For more information on shamanic fire ceremony, visit the Four Winds blog:

http://thefourwinds.com/blog/the-shaman-and-relationships/ fire-ceremony

Grounding

When I sit in the park near my home enjoying open space while overlooking Manhattan, I find it hard to imagine millions of people inhabiting that small island. So many spend their days going from an apartment high above the ground to an office high above the ground and back again, touching the concrete of the sidewalks with their thick-soled shoes only long enough to get from one place to the next. In other cities, while the buildings may not be as tall, people spend most of their time moving from their climatically controlled homes to their climatically controlled cars to their schools or offices and back again. In doing this, we miss out on the nourishment of nature. Nature is like a vitamin we have to take regularly to experience true well-being. In the way that we often don't get enough Vitamin D from the sun in the winter and our bodies become depleted, when we don't breathe fresh air, feel soft ground under our feet or listen to the breeze moving through the trees, we also become physically depleted, spiritually disconnected and mentally ungrounded.

A friend of mine sends her son to a school where they spend the first two hours of every day in the forest, exploring and playing in nature. Can you imagine how many fewer cases of attention deficit disorder would be treated with medication if all children were given time to move their bodies in a space that's free of technology, jarring noises and distractions?

Most of us spend our time trying to fit into the box we've been assigned to rather than trying to get out of it. Most of us have never even been to a working farm, much less grown our own food. We haven't walked barefoot on the ground or touched the soil with our hands in years. On a daylong retreat I led in upstate New York, one of my students said, "I like nature, I just don't want it to get too close to me."

Who can blame her? Nature can be unpredictable and scary. In fact, just before she arrived for the retreat, I heard a knocking sound outside the house we were renting in the Catskill Mountains. Even though we were in the middle of nowhere, my first thought was that someone was trying to break into our car. When I looked out the window, I saw a huge mama bear up on her hind legs pounding on the door of the shed where the garbage cans were kept. Two of her bear cubs stood on all fours behind her, and the smallest one watched from its perch in a nearby tree. I called for my husband and we watched them for about twenty minutes.

At first I was frightened, but as I continued watching I saw myself in this mama bear. She pulled all the garbage out of the cans, parceled it out to her cubs and then tried to find something for herself to eat. She was just a big furry mama bear taking care of her babies. This doesn't mean she wouldn't have tried to make me into a meal if she was hungry enough or if I'd threatened her cubs, but she wasn't rabid or terrifying.

So many of us have been taught not to get dirty, to fear the creatures of the natural world and to try to bring order to that which appears to be chaotic. When we go into the forest, nothing is organized in perfectly straight lines like we see in landscaped parks, but there *is* a natural order to everything, whether we recognize it or not. The intelligence of the universe creates an order that's beyond our comprehension.

In the shamanic tradition, Pacha Mama, Mother Earth, is worshipped with as much reverence as Father Sky. One is not more deified than the other. They work together to create balance in the universe. Through our Western religious model, we've learned that Earth is a place where we work out our karma so that we can then enter a better place, which is called heaven. When we picture heaven as a place up in the clouds that we're trying to get to, we miss out on the beauty that's all around us. And in doing this over time, we destroy what's been given to us right here on Earth. My personal belief is that the Earth will always restore herself to balance—it just may not be pleasant for her inhabitants and may take a long time.

In a "key practice text" from Plum Village called the Five Earth Touchings, Thích Nhất Hạnh puts forth the importance of grounding to our spiritual life. In one of these "touchings," he writes, "I see that I am whole, protected, and nourished by this land and all of the living beings who have been here and made life easy and possible for me ... I see myself touching my ancestors of Native American origin who have lived on this land for such a long time and known the ways to live in peace and harmony with nature, protecting the mountains, forests, animals, vegetation, and minerals of this land. I feel the energy of this land penetrating my body and soul, supporting and accepting me. I vow to cultivate and maintain this energy and transmit it to future generations."

How We Ground Ourselves

Grounding creates the foundation for our transformational work. Without stability, without connection to the Earth, the changes we undergo can overwhelm us. Connecting to the Earth and nature is one of the most potent ways to ground. We can also create more grounding through yoga, meditation and deep breathing. The following practices will help you feel more grounded, less caught in your head and more present in your body, whether you're in a high-rise apartment building, in an underground office with no windows or on a boat at sea.

Yoga Poses for Grounding

Yoga helps us create strength and stability within ourselves by working directly with the body, mind and breath. I encourage you to explore these practices as a way to promote the healing of old wounds and create a stable foundation for growing your roots so that you can rise up from them like a strong, healthy oak. Through these practices, you can become as deeply connected to the earth underneath as to the heavens above, rooted in your own stability and able to provide shade and shelter for the people around you.

While a structure won't stand without a stable foundation, it also won't withstand the winds of change without fluidity. So we need to create strength and stability in the feet, ankles and legs while also releasing stiffness and rigidity. This sequence of postures focuses on creating strength and stability in the legs while increasing flexibility in the hamstrings and quadriceps. If you're a regular yoga practitioner, feel free to add five or six sun salutations at the beginning of your practice to warm the body and create more intensity for yourself in the standing poses. If you're working with an injury or illness that prevents you from standing, you can modify most poses using a chair.

You'll need a yoga mat and a yoga strap. You can use a long belt or tie if you don't have a strap.

Tadasana: Mountain Pose: This posture teaches us how to stand in our most neutral alignment. In the Yoga Works Methodology, it's called the Blueprint Pose because all other standing postures are variations of this pose. Tadasana is the foundation of our physical strength and stability. If you have trouble standing, you can experience the essence of the pose seated on a chair, simply by sitting upright and focusing on aligning the structure of your body from the ground up.

- Stand barefoot at the front of your yoga mat with your feet together or a few inches apart. Align your toes with the front edge of the mat.
- Press down through the three grounding points on the bottoms of your feet: the ball of the foot at the big toe, the base of the baby toe and the center of the heel.
- Lift the arches of your feet.
- Draw your kneecaps up but not back.
- Draw your inner thighs back and lengthen your tailbone down.
- Lift your abdominal muscles gently in and up.
- Broaden your collarbones and lift the fronts of your armpits while relaxing your shoulder blades down your back.
- Turn your palms forward and reach your fingertips down toward the floor.
- Lift up through the center of the crown of your head (not the forehead).
- Close your eyes and count ten deep breaths. Imagine yourself like a mountain, wide at the base, connected to the Earth and growing up into the heavens.
- Connect to the Earth underneath you. No matter where you stand, the grounding energy of the Earth is always accessible.

Vrksasana: Tree Pose: This pose is the quintessential standing balance pose in yoga practice. It's a wonderful way to connect to your roots by imagining that you become the tree, with its roots growing broad and deep into the earth as its branches stretch upward and out toward the sky. This pose can be done with one hand on the wall. If you can't stand, practice doing the pose mentally and envision your body as a strong and healthy tree swaying in the wind.

- From Tadasana, bring your hands to your hips. Draw your right knee straight up to hip height. Then turn your knee out to the right as far as you can without moving the pelvis.
- Use your right hand to pull your right ankle up to your left inner thigh.

- Place your right heel on your left inner thigh and press inward. If you can't reach the inner thigh, place your heel on your left calf. Avoid pressing your right heel on the inner left knee.
- Bring your palms together in front of your heart while you connect your eyes to a gazing point in front of you.
- Stretch your arms overhead, shoulder distance apart. Reach with your fingertips as if they're the leaves of your tree reaching for the sun.
- Stay focused and do your best to balance for eight deep breaths.
- If you can't balance, put one hand on the wall and reach the other arm up.
- To come out of the pose, point your right knee forward, again at hip height. Bring your hands back to your heart and place your right foot down next to the left.
- Pause in Tadasana, focusing on the qualities of the tree—stability, strength, flexibility, the ability to produce life-force energy and provide shade for other beings.
- Repeat the pose standing on the right foot.
- Incorporate the mantra "I honor my roots as I grow toward my becoming."

Adho Mukha Svanasana: Downward-Facing Dog Pose: This posture stretches the shoulders, neck and back as well as the hamstrings, calves and ankles. It also strengthens the arms, shoulders, back and legs. Downward Dog provides an inversion that tractions the spine, making space between the vertebrae and allowing more space inside the torso for the internal organs. It gently sends fresh blood to the brain, aligning the chakras so that energy can flow effortlessly from the root to the crown.

During countless home practice sessions, my dog Rosie would come over to show me her expert Downward Dog. She appeared to get a rush of pleasure from stretching her whole body in one move. I'm fascinated that no one taught her to do it. It's instinctual, just as the energy of the root chakra is when we begin working with it. Our task as humans is to harness that instinctual energy and send it upward on its path toward the divine. I often teach this pose to beginners or people with illness by having them place their hands on the surface of a sturdy table rather than the floor. This requires less strength from the arms and less flexibility from the hamstrings.

- ⮑ From Tadasana, bend your knees and fold forward.
- ⮑ Plant your hands flat on the floor next to your feet and walk your feet back toward the back of your mat.

- Place your hands shoulder distance apart and your feet hip distance apart.
- Shift your shoulders over your wrists as you would for a push-up. When your heels align over the balls of the feet while the shoulders align over the wrists, you've created the correct distance between your hands and feet for Downward-Facing Dog.
- Bend your knees slightly and shift your hips back and up as far as you can without moving your hands or feet.
- Spread your fingers wide, turning your fingers slightly outward. Press each finger down equally into the earth.
- Fully straighten your arms and draw your hips away from your head.
- Our intention in this pose is to lengthen the spine. If you fully straighten your legs, you may start rounding your lower back, which is counterproductive. Focus more on lifting the hips up and back rather than reaching the heels down.
- Allow your neck to relax, but keep your upper arms working to support your shoulders.
- Spread your toes and point your heels back, directly behind your ankles.
- Hold the pose for eight breaths. Breathe slowly and deeply, closing your eyes and feeling the energy of your hands and feet connecting to the earth. Imagine drawing earth energy up from the palms to the hips as you inhale and down from the hips through the heels as you exhale. Then up from the heels as you inhale and down to the hands as you exhale.
- When you finish, bring your knees gently down for the next pose in the sequence, Balasana (Child's Pose).

Balasana: Child's Pose: This pose stretches the tops of the feet, the knees and the lower back. It calms the nervous system and draws attention inward. This downward-facing fetal position connects us to the experience of being born and the first years of life, to which Muladhara, the root chakra, corresponds. I remember watching my son sleep peacefully in this position, perhaps dreaming that he was back in the safety and darkness of the womb. Even as adults, this pose provides a sense of being held in the womb of Mother Earth.

- From Downward Dog, slowly lower your knees to the floor.
- Separate your knees slightly wider than your hips, keeping your toes together.
- Sit back onto your heels and rest your forehead on the floor.
- If your knees hurt, place a blanket under them. You can also place a block under your buttocks to take pressure off the tops of the feet.
- If your forehead doesn't touch the floor, place the block under it.
- Stay here for as long as you like, a minimum of ten breaths.
- Close your eyes and connect to the nurturing quality of the earth and the warm cocoon the pose creates.
- Incorporate the mantra "I am safe and supported."

Supta Padangusthasana 1 & 2: Reclining Foot to Finger Pose (1 & 2 Variations): This pose is a deep stretch for the hamstrings and inner thigh. The strong sensation of the stretch in the legs and the feeling of resting the back body on the floor give us a deep sense of grounding. These poses can be modified using a strap. I recommend buying a thick yoga strap that's eight feet long. There are several good brands to choose from online. These poses provide a wonderful alternative to the standing poses for anyone whose legs are weak from illness.

- From Balasana (Child's Pose), come to lie down on your back.
- Stretch your left leg out long on the floor and draw your right knee to your chest.
- Keep your head and shoulders resting on the floor comfortably while you wrap your first two fingers around your right big toe and slowly straighten the leg. If you can't straighten the leg with head and shoulders down, place a strap around the ball of your right foot and hold one side of the strap in each hand like you would the reins of a horse.
- If you're holding your big toe, place your left hand on your left thigh to anchor it. If you're holding a strap, keep both elbows off the floor.
- Ground your left inner thigh, reaching through your left heel. Lengthen both sides of your waist.
- Hold the shape for eight breaths, allowing the stretch to be less intense on the inhale and more intense on the exhale.

- If you're using a strap, place both sides of the strap in your right hand.
- Extend your left arm to the left at shoulder height and press your left palm into the floor.
- Roll your right thigh out to the right side as far as you can without lifting your left buttock. Draw your right buttock toward your left inner thigh.
- Reach your tailbone toward your left heel as you flex your left foot.
- Stay for eight breaths, maintaining stability in your pelvis as you stretch. Notice all the energy coursing through your legs. It's the energy of your ancestry, your bloodline.
- Inhale your leg back to center and draw your right knee into your chest before you repeat the pose on the other side. I like to do both variations on each leg twice, finding that I settle in much more the second time.

Apanasana: Downward Energy Pose: This simple pose is great for aiding elimination, which is a function related to the root chakra. It's also a useful way to release the lower back in preparation for relaxation. This pose can be used as a modification for Balasana (Child's Pose). I recommend this as the first pose of the morning for those with chronic lower back pain, which often stems from a sense of instability at the root chakra.

- Lying on your back, simply draw both knees to your chest and interlace your fingers around the shins or hold one wrist.
- As you hug the knees in close, breathe deeply, creating a gentle massage for the lower abdominal area, which houses the intestines.
- Feel the womb you create around yourself in this pose, a protective shell to support you.
- Hold the pose for five to ten breaths until you feel ready for final relaxation.

Savasana: Corpse Pose: You can end every short sequence in this book with Savasana, as it's the traditional way to end a yoga practice. It's interesting to note that all practice, whether gentle or vigorous, whether related to the root chakra or the crown, ends in Corpse Pose, a willing, temporary death. In this pose we can connect with the part of ourselves that's beyond the physical body, that which will remain when our bodies do actually die.

Practicing this pose in relation to the root chakra allows us to become more willing to let go of the tight grip we have on our most basic survival instincts, which is the basic cause for tension in the body and anxiety in the mind. This is the flight-or-fight response. In Savasana, the parasympathetic nervous system takes over and we experience a relaxation response, which creates a deeply calming effect on the mind and a softening effect on the body.

> ⊃ You may want to set an alarm for Savasana in case you fall asleep or if you tend to get anxious about time. This way you'll know you have exactly five, seven or ten minutes, whatever you decide. Five minutes is minimum. Feel free to stay in the pose for as long as fifteen minutes.

- Lie on your mat with your feet hip distance apart, toes rolling out to the sides. If your lower back feels tender, place a rolled blanket under the knees.
- Place your hands by your sides a few inches from the body with your palms facing upward.
- Tuck your shoulder blades under your back so the tops of the shoulders can soften toward the floor.
- Close your eyes and take a deep inhale, and then chant the sound *lam* (as you would chant "*Om*") for the duration of the exhale. *Lam* is the seed mantra for the root chakra. Repeat this eight times.
- Allow your breathing to be natural, with no effort.
- Once you've settled into the position, notice the heaviness of the bones on the floor, the pull that gravity has on the body, the way the muscles relax away from the bones. The heart slows down. Breathing becomes shallower. The body and mind begin to relax.
- Let the Earth support you. Let yourself spread out over the Earth. Imagine your body dissolving into the red, clay earth beneath you. Begin to let go of any identification with yourself as separate. Allow yourself to meld into the space around your physical body. As you become part of the Earth, you understand it, you know its secrets, you're no longer controlled by it, but rather you're naturally in harmony with it.
- When the alarm sounds or you feel ready to finish, take a few deep breaths before you move. Then wiggle your fingers and toes, reconnecting to the parameters of your body. Stretch your arms overhead. Draw your knees into your body and roll to your right side. Come up to sit for a few moments.
- Press your hands to your thighs and chant "*Lam*" nine times. You can choose to end your practice here or move on to meditation.

This sequence of poses will help you become grounded. You'll develop awareness and flexibility in your lower body while connecting to the earth element. Once you finish this sequence, you may want to move on to the walking meditation described in the next section or come into a seated meditation in a chair or on the floor.

Walking Meditation

These words came to me during a silent meditation retreat:

> Lifting, moving, placing, shifting
> With gratitude to sky and rain, earth and legs
> I walk without destination, and with absolute purpose.

Most of the time we think of walking as a means to an end, as a way to get from Point A to Point B. Even walking as a form of exercise is a means to an end. We're walking so that we can become more physically fit. In walking meditation, we slow down this habitual activity of placing one foot in front of the other so that we can investigate. In slowing down we see the underlying mechanics of getting from one place to another. As with traditional seated meditation where we follow the breath, we follow our steps to bring our attention into the present moment. For our specific purposes of grounding, we'll place a strong emphasis on the connection of our feet to the Earth and the energetic quality of groundedness.

Formal Practice:

It's best to begin walking meditation in a space at least fifteen feet long. If you need to practice inside and you live in small quarters, you can use the hallway of your apartment building or the roof. I prefer practicing outside in the park. If you have a yard or a park near your home, go there. Connecting to actual ground—grass, soil, earth— is more stabilizing than the floor of your home or the roof of your building. If you can safely do this practice barefoot, your connection to the Earth will be even more powerful.

Before you begin, stand tall in Tadasana (Mountain Pose) and take a few deep breaths, feeling your body exactly where it is. When you're ready to begin moving, say to yourself, "Now I begin walking meditation."

Then just say to yourself what you are doing: "Lifting right foot, moving right foot, placing right foot, shifting forward. Lifting left foot, moving left foot, placing left foot, shifting forward." I learned these cues from my teacher Sarah Powers. Being very specific about what you're doing will force you to slow down. It's as if you've shot some film of yourself walking and now you're playing it back in slow motion. While you're walking, keep your eyes on the ground about five feet in front of you so that you won't be distracted or strain your neck. Continue with this practice for ten to fifteen steps.

Then pause in Mountain Pose. Take a few deep breaths in and out. Say to yourself, "I am connected to the Earth beneath me." Or, "I am fully supported by the Earth beneath me." Visualize roots growing out from the bottoms of your feet into the Earth, creating great stability for your whole being. Imagine that from these roots you can grow up and out in all directions. These roots can allow you to live life more fully.

Then continue walking very slowly, repeating the phrases of action to yourself for ten to fifteen steps. Once you're in a rhythm, you can just say, "Lifting, moving, placing, shifting." If you notice yourself getting distracted, becoming so comfortable with the words that you're able to say them and still think of other things, slow it down even more. Break down the process of walking even further until you can't think about anything else. This is mind training, but you'll also feel it in your body. It's challenging to move so slowly, and your legs will become fatigued. Try to practice three or four rounds of ten to fifteen steps in one session. This should take about fifteen minutes.

This is a great practice to do before seated meditation, especially if you're feeling anxious, distracted or sluggish. Walking meditation helps you arrive in your body so that when you come to sit in stillness, you're already more centered and able to focus.

Informal Practice:

In addition to the time you set aside specifically for walking meditation, you can practice it during your regular routine. Even if you're walking to get from Point A to Point B you can walk mindfully, without rushing. In New York City, we walk almost everywhere. It can be challenging to pay attention to what we're doing when everyone around us is rushing along, but even when we have to move quickly we can choose to pay attention to our breath and the way our feet feel touching the ground.

Sometimes when I have the urge to start texting someone while I'm walking, I take a deep breath instead and visualize that person in my mind and just say silently, "I am thinking of you right now and wishing you happiness and peace." They may not know consciously at that moment that I'm thinking of them, but they'll feel it on some level.

Also while walking faster you can practice a simpler version of meditation by just noting your steps and your breath. You can say to yourself, "Inhale, step, step, step. Exhale, step, step, step," noting how many steps you take as you inhale and how many you take as you exhale. Or you can say, "Inhale, right, left, right. Exhale, left, right, left." Sometimes this version makes me feel like I'm in the Army, but in a way that's the kind of training we're doing, training ourselves to be grounded in our experience and in sync with the world around us. In Army training, soldiers learn discipline, honor and unity with their fellow soldiers. These are some of the core values of the root chakra, which is the energy center most connected to our feet and legs and to our work of forgiveness, letting go and grounding.

Ultimately, you have to make the practice your own. Experiment with different forms of walking meditation and find a way that works for you. Then stick with it for a while until you feel at home in the practice. When you start to feel too comfortable, change something so that you're always challenging yourself to remain present. Trungpa Rinpoche used to give very specific instructions for meditation to his Western students. Then just about the time that they started to get comfortable with the instructions, even slightly complacent, he'd change them. This is the practice. It's not about getting comfortable or mastering walking meditation so that we can move on to something else. It's about learning how to continually arrive in the present moment with a reverence for the support of the Earth beneath us and the life unfolding around us.

The Essence of Forgiveness, Letting Go and Grounding

When we're able to practice forgiveness we become lighter, happier beings, able to be at peace with ourselves and to honor one another. When we continually practice the art of letting go, nothing can impede us on our path of transformation. As Steve Maraboli writes in his book *Unapologetically You: Reflections on Life and the Human Experience*, "The truth is, unless you let go, unless you forgive yourself, unless you forgive the situation, unless you realize that the situation is over, you cannot move forward." When we're truly grounded, we aren't overwhelmed by what's new. We have the capacity for change.

I encourage you to incorporate all these tools into your daily life for a while and notice what shifts and changes for you. Notice what most supports you and enables you to grow. Ultimately, you are your own teacher, the tender of your own garden. You have the power to make it as lush and beautiful as you choose.

CHAPTER 3

Shadows Can Be Seen
Only in the Light

**"Shadow is a colour as light is, but less brilliant;
light and shadow are only the relation of two tones."**
— Paul Cézanne, *Letters*

One hot summer day when I was about three years old, my parents took me to the St. Louis Zoo. All the unfamiliar animals must have sparked my observation skills, because at some point I looked down and noticed a dark spot on the ground in the shape of a little girl. I started to walk away, but it followed me. I panicked and sprinted toward my father, screaming, "It's following me! It's following me!" I jumped into the safety of his arms and caught my breath as he tried to figure out what had been following me. "It's your shadow," my mother said with a smile. "Everybody has one. See." She pointed to her own. "It can't hurt you if you're not scared of it." For the rest of the day I kept looking back to see if my shadow was still there until eventually the sun started setting and it faded away.

As my wise mother pointed out, we all have a shadow, but we can see it only when we step into the light. Most of us try to hide our shadow in the darkness. We think that if others see our greed, our jealousy, our anger or our addiction, they'll judge or reject us for not being good enough. Eventually we start to hide the shadow even from ourselves. Then when we meet someone who's greedy, jealous, angry or an addict, we judge them harshly, not recognizing that the reason they push our buttons is that they're bringing our shadow into the light.

In our modern electrified world, we value light over darkness. We think of the darkness as an inconvenience to be remedied. We've forgotten that only in the darkness can we rest, only in the darkness can we witness the beauty of the cosmos with its billions of stars and constellations.

When people attend my retreats in a remote location, they're always astounded by how many stars they can see in the sky. They're also quite surprised to find themselves going to bed earlier and waking up earlier. Without the stimulation of television and ambient light, they attune with nature's rhythmic exchange of darkness and light.

On a family vacation to Big Sur, my husband, who generally watches television until midnight every night, went in to check out a room before we booked it for the night. "There's only one problem," he said when he came out. "No TV."

"Hallelujah!" I replied, looking forward to reading a book in the quiet of the wilderness.

Our son fell asleep at about seven o'clock that night, and when I looked over at my husband forty-five minutes later, he too was fast asleep, with his book resting on his chest. Instead of avoiding the darkness like we often do at home—answering one more e-mail, watching one more episode of a television show—he let go into the darkness and was able to get the best night's sleep he'd had in years.

Most of the time we behave like my three-year-old self, running from our shadow, forgetting that it can't hurt us if we aren't scared of it. Not knowing that our shadow can be our greatest teacher. When we're able to face the parts of ourselves that we've exiled for being unacceptable, we can begin to integrate them and experience a deeper sense of wholeness.

When We Deny Our Shadow

When we deny our shadow side—the feelings of not having enough, not being enough, our jealousy, confusion and fear—these natural thoughts and emotions can turn into self-doubt, self-destruction, manipulation of others and compulsive behavior.

The same year I discovered my physical shadow, I began dancing with my mental shadow. Back in the days when you could leave your child in the car alone for five minutes while you ran into the dry cleaners, my mother once warned me not to eat the Easter candy she'd just bought at the grocery store while I waited in the car for her. When she came back to the car, she said I looked like a chipmunk preparing for hibernation, my cheeks filled with Cadbury eggs and marshmallow Peeps.

"I told you not to eat that candy," she said.

I could barely speak with my mouth so full. "I wasn't eating it," I said. "I was just holding it in my mouth."

Rather than being given one or two pieces of candy to savor, I'd been given a warning not to touch it, which only fueled my curiosity. I knew that if my mother saw me eating the candy I'd be in trouble, so rather than denying myself the pleasure, I tried to hide it. When I got caught, I tried to justify it.

Before Kripalu became a center for holistic wellness, it was an ashram headed by the charismatic yogi Amrit Desai. As recounted by Stephen Cope in his book *Yoga and the Quest for the True Self*, Desai had an electrifying presence. He could turn a room of three hundred yogis into a beaming ball of light. But his shadow turned out to be just as massive as his light. Eventually, several female devotees came forth to report his sexual misconduct, which shook the foundation of the spiritual organization so profoundly that Kripalu transformed from a religious community practicing abstinence while working to transcend the shadow side into a holistic learning community geared toward integrating both the darkness and the light through many faiths, practices and philosophies.

How We Work with the Shadow

As I learned from running from my own shadow at the zoo, we can never truly get rid of our shadow. Our work is to turn toward the shadow and see what it has to teach us. Buddhist teachings are laden with stories of integrating the shadow. Take Milarepa. He was born into a prosperous family with good parents. As he was still a young child when his father fell ill, his inheritance was left in the care of his aunt and uncle until he turned eighteen. His father had asked them to take care of Milarepa and his mother, but greed got the best of them. They took all the money for themselves and forced Milarepa and his mother to work in the fields and live in poverty.

When Milarepa came of age, his mother tried unsuccessfully to get their money back. Finally, in desperation she sent Milarepa to learn black magic, hoping he could destroy the aunt and uncle and they could get their money back. Though he was an excellent student, learning quickly how to wreak havoc on his enemies, the black magic caused more harm to his family than good and forced Milarepa into exile.

Eventually he met a spiritual teacher who taught him that revenge was a fruitless pursuit and that the only worthwhile path was one in which he accepted *all* of life and his circumstances while cultivating inner peace.

The story of his enlightenment goes that one night he came home to find his house full of demons eating his food and drinking his tea. When he asked them to leave, they didn't listen. When he tried explaining the spiritual teachings, they ignored him. Eventually, he burst into a rage and commanded them to leave. They all paused and looked at him as if he was crazy before laughing and going back to their feast. Finally, he surrendered to them. He realized they weren't going to leave and he knew *he* wasn't going to leave. After he sat down and made peace with them, all but one vanished. This last one, the nastiest demon, had been stalking him his whole life. He knew he couldn't run away anymore, so instead he opened the demon's mouth and stuck his head inside. Thanks to that act of true surrender, the demon vanished and Milarepa was free.

It's not until we're willing to fully face our shadow that it ceases to control us. Not until we're willing to acknowledge our greed, our fear, our jealousy or our deceitfulness will it lose its power over us. We all have a story like Milarepa's. Each one of us has felt banished somehow from the soft, sweet place of love that is our birthright. We've all tried by circuitous routes to get back to that sweetness. Eventually, we realize that all the methods that cause suffering for ourselves and others are fruitless. Then we have to sit down with the demons and tell them that we aren't going to leave our home no matter what. Because our misery is their food, eventually they'll get hungry and leave, recognizing that we'll no longer be feeding them.

We can do this through dialogue. When you notice that one of your "demons" has taken over, rather than running away or trying to fight it, talk to it. Ask the demon:

- Why have you come?
- What do you need?
- What do you have to show me or teach me?
- How can I help you be free from suffering?

What we most often find is that the demons are just like our physical shadow, parts of ourselves that we've ignored. The demon of compulsive eating may in fact be the part of you that's longing for the love and comfort you haven't allowed yourself to have for many years. So instead you've been seeking to satiate your heart with food. The demon of jealousy may be the part of you that desperately needs your own approval. We're jealous of someone else only when we believe that who we are and what we have aren't good enough.

Once we recognize these demons and understand why they've come, they will transform from sources of suffering to indicators of when we're out of balance. We can use them to understand how to best take care of ourselves.

For many years, the demon of compulsive eating stalked me and pillaged both my inner and outer home. Not until I recognized that this demon dressed up as sugary cereal and cheese pizza was actually the part of me I had exiled for not being perfect was I finally able to let it go. This is when I began replacing midnight snacks with self-approval. And slowly, over time, the demon turned into an ally. Now if I feel the urge to sneak food, I ask myself, "What's really going on here?" The answer is never about doughnuts or pasta. Asking this first question helps me to turn toward myself rather than turn *on* myself. I can then ask, "What need am I not acknowledging?" or "What part of myself do I not want to see?" Most often, the answer is that I'm tired or lonely, scared or sad.

In asking these kinds of questions, we let go of punishing ourselves and begin honoring ourselves. We become better friends to ourselves and we are then able to be better friends to others. We all carry darkness inside us that we try to hide, but when we bring it out into the light, it no longer has the power to control us.

Stepping into the Light

"Our deepest fear is not that we are inadequate. Our deepest fear is that we are powerful beyond measure. It is our light, not our darkness, that most frightens us. We ask ourselves, 'Who am I to be brilliant, gorgeous, talented, and fabulous?' Actually, who are you not to be? You are a child of God. Your playing small does not serve the world. There is nothing enlightened about shrinking so that other people will not feel insecure around you. We are all meant to shine, as children do. We were born to make manifest the glory of God that is within us. It's not just in some of us; it's in everyone. And as we let our own light shine, we unconsciously give others permission to do the same." — Marianne Williamson, *A Return to Love: Reflections on the Principles of A Course in Miracles*

Why We Fear Stepping into the Light

I recently saw a YouTube video in which several women were standing around complaining about their hair, their thighs and various other aspects of their appearance. They took turns, as if passing the talking stick in a sacred ceremony. When the last woman's turn to demean herself arrived, she didn't speak. The others were shocked, and when the silent woman walked away, they started demeaning her behind her back. "Who does she think she is? Better than us?"

It was meant to be funny, but I found it very depressing. Somewhere between cartoons and puberty, most young women pick up the dangerous and detrimental habit of self-judgment. They learn with their friends to speak out their perceived inadequacies as a way of fitting in. In her song "32 Flavors," Ani DiFranco sings, "God help you if you are an ugly girl, but too pretty is also your doom, for everyone harbors a secret hatred for the prettiest girl in the room."

This mode of thinking keeps the pack together. Nobody rises too far above. Nobody is allowed to sink too far below. DiFranco goes on to sing "God help you if you are a phoenix and you dare to rise up from the ash. A thousand eyes will smolder with jealousy as you were just flying past."

From what I've witnessed, young men do this in a different way. Rather than talking about their shortcomings, they compete with one another. Then whoever wins sets the tone and the unspoken rules for the pack.

Stepping into the light often means breaking free from the pack. Sometimes we'll dare to be a phoenix and other times we won't. However, I believe it's these moments of daring that lead us to our destiny.

In seventh grade we had twin day at school. Everyone partnered up with a best buddy and agreed on a matching outfit and, for the girls, a hairstyle they would wear that day.

My twin was Julie, who sat next to me in math class. She used canes to walk, and her knees buckled inward, forcing her to lead with her head to gain momentum during the rush between classes, but she often arrived late to class anyway, disheveled and moody. She spoke with a soft, slow slur that was tedious for a room of twelve-year-olds to listen to, but I had a brother at home with a brain injury, and he also walked very slowly and spoke the same way. It was so familiar to me that I really didn't think much about it. Most of the other kids knew better than to be directly mean to her, but they often made fun of her behind her back. Even the nicer ones said things like, "If she wasn't so mean, I'd be nice to her." I could understand why they felt that way, but through taking care of my brother, my mother had taught me a lot about compassion. She pointed out that when someone is suffering, they're not always going to be nice. She said we have to forgive them and be nice to them anyway.

I remember how grumpy I felt when, after breaking my leg, I had to use crutches for six weeks, but I knew it was a finite inconvenience. Julie didn't have that light at the end of the tunnel. She was stuck with the crutches indefinitely. But I'll be honest: Did I really want to dress like twins with her? No, I wanted to dress up like twins with the cool kids. But we both had these red and white striped shirts from The Gap, these white jean shorts and this long blond hair, and in my heart I knew what was right.

I'm not going to pretend I walked into the school full of pride that day, especially when I saw my other friends paired up and giggling. I felt hot, slightly embarrassed and then guilty for feeling embarrassed. I just wanted to blend in, but there we were, most definitely not blending. Yet I remember seeing Julia's face light up when she walked into math class and saw me wearing my side ponytail just like hers. It was worth any discomfort I was feeling.

Looking back as an adult, I see that, yes, I helped her feel a sense of belonging on that day that she most likely didn't feel much of the time. But she actually helped me so much more than I helped her, by teaching me to be humble and patient, to let go of my ego, to not follow the crowd or worry about gaining approval from others. And when I see the photos from that day, I think we really were so much more alike than we were different—just two preteen girls trying to get through middle school, looking for someone and something to mirror back to us the goodness, the lovable nature and the beauty that we couldn't always see for ourselves.

The light itself is not personal. It shows us both our grandeur and our wretchedness. We fear the light not only because it might show us that we're better than we thought we were but also that we don't measure up to the impossible standards we've set for ourselves. An ex-boyfriend of mine used to say jokingly, "Hey, look at how great I am! But if you really think I'm great, you must be an idiot."

Have you ever received a standing ovation? Have you ever been booed by the crowd? It's interesting that both of these experiences conjure up a huge amount of energy, which is uncomfortable for us to endure. Both praise and criticism carry charges that we must be willing to experience if we are to step into our own light.

How We Step into the Light

The practice of stepping into the light is one we must do in the company of others. Sure, we can sit in front of the mirror and tell ourselves we're wonderful and beautiful and brave—it helps get things started—but this doesn't automatically translate into the ability to do that in the presence of others, where we risk judgment and rejection.

When I was eight years old, I would tease my hair up into a side ponytail and use the top of a bedpost as a microphone to sing Whitney Houston songs over and over for an audience of stuffed animals and dolls. I was fearless and fabulous in the privacy of my bedroom, but when I auditioned for the summer musical theater, singing "A Few of My Favorite Things" for the judges, I tanked. The pressure of performing for others drowned out my inherent ability to sing and my desire to entertain. For me, as for many others, this has been a lifelong challenge—taking the light I know is inside me out into the world, risking judgment, daring the possibility of failure, flirting with the notion of success.

One practice that's helped me prepare for the continual auditions of life is something I call "The Circle of Success." This is a Body/Mind Reconditioning exercise to get us into the mental and physical state that allows us to tap into our inherent confidence in situations where we might otherwise run away or freeze in fear. I originally learned a version of this exercise in my training to become a neurolinguistic programming (NLP) practitioner. NLP is a huge body of techniques used to help people build rapport, release bad habits and create more success in their lives. I've adapted and simplified a few of the exercises I learned in that training to suit the needs of my clients and students, which I now include in my Body/Mind Reconditioning work.

Body/Mind Reconditioning Exercise:
The Circle of Success

- ➲ Stand tall with your eyes closed and remember a time when you felt very confident and successful. Perhaps you'd just won a sporting competition or received public praise from your boss. Stand the way you stood, breathe the way you breathed, imagine that you're wearing what you had on at the time and that people are celebrating you.

- ➲ Imagine a golden circle of light around you on the floor, with a soft pleasant humming sound, encircling this self-confidence. Feel the sense of accomplishment. Take it all in.

- ➲ Step outside the circle, leaving the confidence inside.

- ➲ Imagine a time in the future when you want to feel confident and experience great success. Think of the moment right before you step up to the podium to speak, step onto the court to play or show up for that first date with a new person.

- ➲ Step back into the golden circle, hear the hum and immerse yourself in these confident, fabulous feelings. Let self-confidence flood your body and mind. See yourself filled with confidence as you give your speech, take your shot or speak to that new person.

- ➲ Step back out of the circle, bringing the confident, successful feelings with you.

- ➲ You can now take these feelings into any situation, anywhere you go. This exercise works best if you have a specific situation in mind. When the actual situation arrives, take a few moments beforehand to do this exercise again. I guarantee you'll tap into a vibrant energy that will cause your light to shine bright.

Recently I attended a sacred women's circle where we practiced doing the opposite of what the women on the YouTube video I mentioned did. We sat facing one another with bowls of chocolate, rose petals and marshmallows to represent the sweetness of life and ourselves. Then we spoke out to the group something we like about ourselves as we threw some of the sweetness into the center of the circle. I remember saying, "Often when I look in the mirror, I actually think I am pretty." I was surprised at how nervous I was to admit this to the group. After the first few rounds, it got easier. Women started declaring their intelligence, their success at work, their special talents and gifts, even their sexual prowess. We laughed together and cheered for one another. We all left feeling more connected to our own light and feeling that we had permission to share it with others. This is something I'd like to teach to middle school girls. When we break the habit of group self-condemnation and embrace the practice of group self-praise, we set ourselves and our peers on the path toward a future filled with light.

When we find ourselves in situations that offer us the opportunity to step into the light, we often notice that resistance and self-judgment arise almost simultaneously. To let go of this resistance and to release this self-judgment, we can ask ourselves these simple questions:

- What's the worst thing that could happen if I risk stepping into the light at this moment?
- What's the best thing that could happen?
- What might I miss out on if I don't?
- What might I gain if I do?

We all have these opportunities every day. We can present our business card to someone we overhear talking about how they need the exact skills that we possess. We can volunteer to lead the choir at church on Sunday. We can audition for the community theater that we've been dreaming of joining for years. We can take a new class, offer to speak first, ask for what we want and declare our goodness to the world. When we do this, we aren't trying to put ourselves above others—we're demonstrating that it's okay for them to bring their own unique light into the world as well.

Pleasure and Pain

In working with our shadow and our light, we come upon the yin and yang of our daily experience: pleasure and pain. We naturally gravitate toward pleasure and avoid pain. However, we have a guilt-based relationship with pleasure, while we tend to venerate those who intentionally seek out pain. For example, a commercial for a certain brand of chocolate referred to the product as a "guilty" pleasure. Why do we have to feel guilty for enjoying a little chocolate? Conversely, we see endurance athletes as heroes for intentionally enduring pain and pushing their bodies to the limits to win a race.

Because pleasure is often viewed as sinful or naughty, we try to deny ourselves. Then, rather than having one piece of chocolate and enjoying it, we have twenty and feel awful, both physically and emotionally. I believe this is one of the major causes of obesity in the world today. Data from the National Health and Nutrition Examination Survey from 2009 and 2010 found that more than two in three adults are considered to be overweight or obese, while more than one in twenty adults are considered to be extremely obese. Also, about a third of children and adolescents ages six to nineteen are considered to be overweight or obese. Sugary foods, foods high in fat and salt, and processed carbohydrates are physically addictive, but that's not the only problem. Cultural taboos around experiencing pleasure, combined with lack of conscious awareness of our bodies and our propensity toward self-condemnation, also play a big part in these disturbingly high numbers.

My college roommate's father was a grocer, so she'd been around lots of food all her life. I marveled that some days she ate a salad for lunch and other days she ate a McDonald's Big Mac with fries. She appeared to be unabashedly eating exactly what she wanted when she was hungry and stopping when she was full. This was as foreign to me as wearing a kimono and performing formal tea service.

When I went to the grocery store, I checked every label for calories and fat. I bought the things that I thought would keep me thin and denied myself many of the things I really wanted. But at midnight, after a day of being "good," I'd open the pantry and see my rice cakes next to my roommate's Ferrero Rocher and I couldn't control myself. I'd scarf down several of her chocolate treats and hope she wouldn't notice before I had a chance to replace them.

Eventually she did notice, to my great shame. But instead of making me feel worse for being a thief *and* a glutton, she told me she was going to hide some treats for me in a brown paper bag every week in the back of the pantry so I could sneak them without actually stealing them. This is still one of the nicest things anyone has ever done for me. She didn't force me out of my hiding place. She gave me permission not only to enjoy the chocolates but also to honor myself and the place where I was emotionally at that time. I believe her act of kindness helped me eventually stop sneaking food and hiding my desire for pleasure from myself and the world.

When I first learned from conscious-eating guru Geneen Roth that it was possible to enjoy a few squares of chocolate in the light of day and then to stop and move on with the day, I was dumbfounded. No one had ever taught me about bringing consciousness to eating. I had learned about deprivation and overindulgence, about calorie and fat content, but never about the simple pleasure that comes from savoring a single scoop of cherry-vanilla ice cream. "We don't want to *eat* hot fudge sundaes as much as we want our lives to *be* hot fudge sundaes," Roth writes in her book *Women, Food and God: An Unexpected Path to Almost Everything.* "We want to come home to ourselves." In giving ourselves permission to enjoy pleasure, we invite more of who we are to come home.

We all derive pleasure from a variety of sources, and many of life's pleasures are healthy in moderation, but our culture does not condone moderation. It's something we have to cultivate and practice. Even the Buddha, after living a life of opulence and then one of extreme deprivation, had to learn the hard way that the middle way is the path to happiness.

Addictions to alcohol, drugs, sex and even violence come from our unwillingness to address our real needs, our inability to show up and care for ourselves deeply. Much of the time this is because we weren't taught how to care for ourselves emotionally and spiritually by those who cared for us physically as children. But it can also be a forgetting. Perhaps at one point in our lives we felt loved, we felt cherished, we felt that we did know how to take care of our own needs, and then, due to circumstances or relationships, we forgot and we need to be reminded.

Eating Meditation

One way of developing a healthy relationship to pleasure is through eating meditation. All of us eat every day, but most of the time we're distracted, whether by socializing, the Internet or work. We rarely stop and make the act of eating the focal point of our experience.

I first learned eating meditation on a silent retreat with Geneen Roth. As a former food addict, I found it to be one of the most challenging meditations to practice regularly. However, when I do it now it feels like an exquisite gift. It's like I've stopped running and realized that the only thing chasing me was my own shadow. Not only is it a relief to stop running, but it also makes the experience of eating a great joy. Even if you don't have emotional issues with food, you may have digestive issues or simply a sense that you could be eating better and taking better care of yourself. This practice is extremely useful in cultivating presence and aiding in digestion and absorption of food.

When I don't want to do it and I inquire into this resistance, I'm surprised by what comes up. It used to be the fear that if I paid close attention to my eating, I would enjoy it so much that it would be even more difficult to let go when the meal was over. But actually, the opposite is true. When we're truly present with anything we do, especially those acts that bring us pleasure, we find that less becomes more because we're so fully absorbed in the experience.

The resistance I feel now comes more from a fear of being bored or lonely. These are the feelings that were hiding beneath the compulsion.

Yet when I eat quickly or when I eat just to fill my belly and get on with the next thing, I don't experience the pleasure I'm seeking. I often end up eating more in search of that pleasure only to find that it isn't there. This is the basic habit that leads to binge eating. Slow, mindful eating creates the opposite effect.

Unless you're on a retreat with like-minded people, it can be difficult to practice eating mediation in the company of others. I remember a smart and kind woman who attended one of my yoga retreats two years in a row and had released a significant amount of weight in the year between. During the second retreat, I noticed that after she filled her plate, she sat down slowly, placed it in front of her and closed her eyes for a few moments before picking up her fork. She ate slowly and quietly, to the point where her friend jokingly commented on it. It seemed that the woman's mindfulness made her friend uncomfortable because it highlighted her own shadow side. She didn't let the jokes derail her. She chewed her food. She breathed. She ate dessert and left some of it on her plate. I imagine this was one of the most important practices in helping her come to a healthy weight.

I'll explain the more formal practice you can do when you're eating alone or on retreat as well as the quick informal practice you can do when you're dining with others. I also challenge you to ask yourself:

- Do I always feel like I have to eat with others?
- Do I tend to feel like I need to be alone with my food?

Either can be limiting. When we're able to establish a firm ground within ourselves, we can allow the outer circumstances to change without feeling as if we're being sabotaged. This practice is one of the most effective ways to establish that ground. Even if you can do it only in the morning with your cup of coffee and a handful of granola, you'll find that learning to savor your food and pay attention to the process of eating will help you let go of the tight grip that causes most addictions to arise.

Eating meditation is exceedingly useful to practice because eating is something we all do every day. When we bring mindfulness to any daily activity, we're more likely to bring mindfulness into the rest of our experiences.

Formal Practice:

It's wonderful to prepare your own food at home for this practice, but if you're at a restaurant, you can improvise and still gain deep benefit.

Begin this practice by first becoming aware of the sensation of hunger in your body. Where do you feel hunger? Is it in the lower abdomen or the upper abdomen? Do you feel it more as growling or stabbing, as nausea or just emptiness? (If you begin this meditation and you realize that you aren't actually hungry, that you're just craving food, you can simply bring awareness to the experience of craving for a while and you'll most likely find that the awareness will help it dissipate so that you can move on to other activities and come back to eating meditation when you're actually hungry.)

Once you've established that you're experiencing hunger and you're very aware of what it feels like, close your eyes and place one hand on the abdomen and ask your body what would be most nourishing at this time. If you already have a meal planned, you might make slight variations depending on what your body signals. I get signals of color and texture that almost always indicate what my body actually needs. If I see the color yellow, I know that my body is craving yellow bell pepper or a similar yellow or orange vegetable. I can also usually feel if my body is in need of lighter foods, like fruit or salad, or heavier foods, like cooked veggies and rice. I find this method of choosing food to be much more effective than setting up hard and fast rules for myself. In trying to stick to them, I'll inevitably break those rules when they aren't in alignment with what my body needs.

A friend of mine struggled to be a vegetarian for eight years, slowly depleting her body. Finally, she went to visit a Tibetan monk and healer who told her that in his tradition meat is used as medicine and that she was in need of this kind of medicine. Seeing meat as medicine allowed her to relax her rigid rules and give her body what it actually needed. Now she eats meat once or twice a month in a ceremonial way, around the time of menstruation, to give her body the nutrients it needs to maintain a healthy hormonal cycle.

Once you've established what your body wants, if you're going to the grocery store to buy the ingredients, you can extend your meditation to the processes of choosing produce, walking through the aisles or standing in line at the checkout. All these acts are sacred, and usually we do them alone, making it easier to be mindful. If you find yourself shopping with a wild four-year-old running around putting boxes on his head, invite that into the meditation, too. Any meditation is about showing up to be with what is.

Once you get home and step into the kitchen, you can say a quick prayer: "May I be present with myself and with the food I am now preparing." Then begin to mindfully place your ingredients on the counter. Feel the skin of the veggies. Notice the weight of your knife. Look at the texture of the cutting board. Hear the running water as you fill your pot with water. Whatever actions you take in preparing the food can be done with great care and attention. Notice when your mind strays or when you speed up. When this happens, simply bring your attention back to your actions and take a few deep breaths to help you slow down.

I love watching cooking shows with real chefs who don't seem to even notice how time-consuming it is to add all the intricate touches to the food they cook. Even though they know it will take only a few minutes to eat and they may not even be the one who will eat it, they give so much care and attention because they love the act of cooking. We can love what we're doing, too. Even if we aren't exceptional chefs, there's a natural skill within each of us to prepare nourishing food for ourselves and others.

If you're cooking your food and it requires time unattended, you can take a seated meditation either on your meditation cushion or sitting in a kitchen chair. Simply sit up tall and follow the breath. From time to time you can listen for the water boiling or the timer on the oven ticking. Notice if you become anxious, wanting the food to be ready more quickly, or if you become bored and start to distract yourself with other things. Let this process of feeding yourself be a priority. Nourishing ourselves with the food that our bodies need when we're hungry is a great act of compassion and kindness.

When the food finishes cooking and you're making the final touches, notice how you place the food on your plate, what silverware you choose. I discovered through this practice that I always chose a small bowl or plate and a small spoon and fork as a way of trying to keep myself small. After this realization I was shocked to recognize the many other ways I tried to keep myself small. But this prompted me to start consciously working with that desire to be small. I realized that it was in essence a desire to be cared for, the way a mother cares for a child, and that experiencing that care had nothing to do with the size of my bowl or spoon. It had to do with my willingness to care for myself and let others support me as well.

You may notice the opposite, that you always choose the largest bowl or cup or plate, to make sure you get your fair share. That's not wrong, but when we bring awareness to these automatic choices, we can release the ones that don't serve us and make different choices that are in service of our well-being.

Once you've served yourself, sit quietly for a few moments observing the food before you eat. See it, smell it, feel the warmth of it wafting toward you. Then you can say a prayer that feels meaningful to you. This is what I say: "May this food be to the nourishment of my being so that I may be free from suffering and of service to others. I gratefully acknowledge every being that provided me with this food. I thank the land and the rain, the sun and the sky for creating this food. May all beings everywhere be fully nourished and free from suffering."

Then begin to eat. Notice the first bite in your mouth, the temperature and texture of the food. Notice how if feels to chew the food and to swallow it. Try putting down your fork or spoon as you chew so that the next bite isn't automatic but rather intentional. Notice the feeling of the food arriving in your stomach. Your brain will receive the message that your stomach is filling up more quickly and clearly when you pay full attention.

When you get to the point where you've been nourished by the food and it's time to stop eating, notice the emotional quality. I always feel slightly sad at the end of a great meal. It's like saying good-bye to my lover. When I feel this way, I say to myself, *I know now that this wonderful meal is over. I'm grateful to have had it, and I'm grateful that another wonderful meal will be available to me the next time I'm hungry.* This helps me let go, trusting myself and my life.

You can extend your mindfulness practice to clearing the table and cleaning the dishes. When you leave the kitchen, try bowing to it in respect of the process but also as a clear indication to yourself that the process, for now, is complete.

Informal Practice:

If this lengthy mindfulness practice feels too overwhelming for you, simply focus your attention during the time when you're chewing your food to become better-acquainted with that actual experience. You can do this even if you're eating a granola bar while walking down the street (which I often find myself doing on busy days). In noticing the chewing, I say to myself, *This, too, is an important moment of my life. I am here now, not yet where I am trying to get to, but right here on the street, chewing my granola bar and walking to my destination.*

When you're eating with others at home or at a restaurant, you can find moments when there are gaps in the conversation and you can really taste the food. Try putting down your fork when you're speaking and between bites when your companion is speaking. Every so often, notice if you are getting full. If you are, even if the food is delicious, pause and remind yourself that you can take it home and have it the next time you're hungry.

I often find that if I'm very hungry when I sit down to eat, I get full quickly, so I often take half my food home, and sometimes I end up eating it a few hours later, sometimes the next day for lunch. Reminding ourselves that we have options and that we can choose the one that's most nourishing allows us to relax even more into the present-moment experience.

Eating meditation is something you can do with your family as well. My son and I say a prayer at the beginning of each meal: "Thank you, Pachamama (Mother Earth), for this food." We talk about the color of the food, the temperature and the taste. Children are very curious about food. They eat what tastes good to them when they're hungry and they stop when they're full. It's tempting to force them to eat more when we think they haven't had enough, but as my friend's pediatrician says, kids won't let themselves starve. If food is available, they'll eat when they're hungry.

My husband tends to become fully engrossed in his thoughts while eating, to the exclusion of everyone else. I try to bring him out a little by asking what he's thinking about while he's eating and how the food tastes. Even these small inquiries can help people become present without feeling judged.

While it's wonderful to offer these practices to others, it's most important that we do this meditation for ourselves so that we can enjoy our experience fully and show others through our actions, not our directions, how to fully embrace the nourishment and pleasure of food and life.

Working with Pain

"When we protect ourselves so we won't feel pain, that protection becomes like armor, like armor that imprisons the softness of the heart." — Pema Chodron, *When Things Fall Apart: Heart Advice for Difficult Times*

We all have a fear of pain. We develop this fear to keep us safe. Our parents teach us not to touch the hot stove or to run with scissors to avoid injury and pain. Yet sometimes we must experience pain to learn how to avoid it in the future. We learn from getting a sunburn that it's better to wear sunscreen. We learn from falling off our bikes how to stay balanced in the future.

At fourteen, I played softball on a team with several friends from school. Our team was very good that year. So was the team we played in our final game of the season. Because it was our last game and it was expected to be a good match, lots of people came to watch. In the fifth or sixth inning, I stepped up to the plate to bat. Although I lacked the discernment to let a bad pitch go by, I almost always made contact with the ball, whether it was a good pitch or not. This time was no different. I swung and smacked the ball into left field. "Run!!" my coach yelled, and I ran as fast as I could to first base. "Keep going!" she shouted. So I rounded second, where I saw the third base coach waving me on. I rounded third and heard the coach scream, "Slide!"

I had no idea how to slide. Maybe I missed that day of practice. I called on memories of watching the Cardinals play at Busch Stadium and did my best to imitate Vince Coleman. I closed my eyes and stuck out my right foot, sliding under the glove of the catcher and into home plate. I heard the umpire yell, "Out!" followed by a loud crack. The crack turned out to be my leg breaking in two places. Luckily, my pants shielded the exposed bones of my lower leg from view. The crowd gasped and I panicked. My mother ran onto the field shouting, "Call 911!"

I couldn't move, so the ambulance had to be driven onto the field. Being moved from the dirt onto a gurney was excruciating, as was every bump we hit while driving off the field. The EMT told me he was sorry that he couldn't give me any pain medicine until we got to the hospital because I was under sixteen. It was a long ride to the hospital, so I had time to both hate him and observe the sensation of a broken leg. It felt like someone had set my leg on fire while twisting the bones in opposite directions.

There's no way I can handle this, I thought. *I'm going to die.* But I didn't die. Per the suggestion of the EMT I hated so much, I took slow deep breaths and began to relax into the pain. I began to feel it as waves of energy coming and going. I realized it wasn't a solid thing that would never go away. I even thought for a moment that this was my body trying to heal itself.

Of course, when we arrived at the hospital I was more than happy to receive the morphine, but having to wait taught me a great lesson about pain. Pain itself cannot kill us. When I gave birth to my son at home, I called on this memory of my broken leg. While much of that experience was a blur, I do remember whispering to my husband, "I'd like some drugs, please." There were none available, so all I could do was breathe and keep letting go until my baby boy came out of my body. At that very moment, I said, "I am never doing that again!" (But I did.)

These experiences of extreme pain, while not something I want to relive on a daily basis, actually empowered me. Knowing I have the capacity to be present with such intense physical sensation gives me the confidence to be present with pain of any kind, especially strong emotions such as fear, grief and rage, without reacting or running away.

In our modern birthing culture, most women are robbed of this empowering experience by well-meaning medical staff who want to help them avoid pain. I gave birth to my second child at the hospital because our insurance in New Jersey doesn't cover home birth, and that experience was much different. As much as I resisted at the beginning, asking for as little intervention as possible, the staff has a way of doing things. The nurses didn't understand why I wouldn't want an IV or continual monitoring of the baby, and they certainly didn't understand why I didn't want an epidural.

After seventeen hours of labor, I pulled my husband's face to mine and said, "Get me the epidural. I can't take it anymore." I thought Nick was going to tell me to ride out this last hour or two, that I was strong and could do it, but to my surprise he nodded and dashed out of the room to find the doctor.

By the time they had the injection ready, my cervix had dilated to nine centimeters. There was no space between contractions for me to hold still so the doctor could put the needle in my spine. It was more painful to try to be motionless than it was to surrender to the natural movements of my body. Eventually, though, I gritted my teeth and held still, and he got the needle in. As the warm sensation slid down my body, I told him he was my favorite of the doctors and then I fell asleep.

When I woke up twenty minutes later, I didn't realize that not only would my legs be numb, but I couldn't move them. So when the time to push came, I felt very disempowered. From their perspective, none of the staff had done anything wrong. They were just doing what they do. But looking back, I wish even one of the nurses had said, "Mommy, you're almost there. You can do this."

Most of my friends who gave birth in traditional settings report the nurses coming in every hour to ask if they were ready for their epidural. While in the midst of a contraction, anyone is going to say yes, but if the medicine isn't available, as it wasn't for me in the ambulance or at home during the birth, we learn how to rely on our bodies and minds to work with pain.

When the laboring mother is undisturbed, her body produces high levels of oxytocin, the love hormone; endorphins, the hormone of pleasure; adrenaline, the hormone of excitement; and prolactin, the hormone that induces mother/baby bonding. When we're given synthetic drugs, these hormones don't work properly and can cause complications such as lack of bonding and postpartum depression. I don't say this to make women feel bad about choosing pain medication during birth. I understand, because I did the same! I say it to point out that the body has a natural inherent wisdom when it comes to dealing with pain and that when we trust in that, it helps us transcend our fears and let go of our resistance so we can tap into a greater power within us than we knew we possessed.

The second chapter of the Yoga Sutras, dedicated to practice, says one of the key ingredients of practice is *tapas*, the ability to endure intensity or pain for the purpose of transformation. If we want to experience true transformation, we'll eventually have to also experience pain. A client of mine who was working on breaking an addiction said to me several times, "I didn't think it was going to be this hard. It is really quite painful." I agreed with her. When we first let go of something that's not serving us, we'll experience the pain of that loss. It may come as physical withdrawal or emotional turmoil, mental agitation or angst, but just like physical pain, it always passes.

Once as she sat in my office sobbing, I encouraged her to watch the waves of emotion, the waves of energy moving through her, noting how it wasn't stagnant but vibrantly alive. This energy was part of the fuel for her transformation. After several experiences of sitting with her strong emotions, she began to trust herself, trusting that the emotions wouldn't kill her, that the sensation would eventually subside and she would be stronger for having gone through it rather than running back to the short-term relief of her addiction.

How Do We Work with Pain?

> Your pain is the breaking of the shell that encloses your understanding.
>
> Even as the stone of the fruit must break, that its heart may stand in the sun, so must you know pain.
>
> And could you keep your heart in wonder at the daily miracles of your life, your pain would not seem less wondrous than your joy. — Kahlil Gibran, *The Prophet*

When you're experiencing mild discomfort or chronic pain, a dialogue can be useful. Ask yourself:

- What sensations am I actually feeling right now?
- What is this pain trying to show/teach me?
- What does this pain have to say?
- How can I best work with this pain without running away or intensifying it?

When working with intense pain, both physical and emotional, it may not be possible to ask yourself questions. The experience becomes more visceral. As in labor and childbirth, it becomes animalistic. All we can do is learn to ride the waves as surfers do. Especially when they crash, if surfers tighten up they'll end up injuring themselves or even drowning, but if they become part of the wave, they can emerge unscathed. This is the art of surrender, one of the other key elements of yoga practice, as described in the Yoga Sutras. We must be willing to endure the intensity, but we must also be willing to surrender to it.

Yoga Poses for Working with Pleasure and Pain

The following yoga poses are helpful in working with pleasure and discomfort as well as connecting to and harnessing the flow of energy that causes sensation and emotion. These poses connect us to the hips and lower belly, home of the Swadisthana chakra, the sacral chakra, which is the energy center related to our shadow and our creative power.

Balasana: Wide-Knee Child's Pose: This pose helps us gently open the pelvis and lower back. It stretches the inner thighs and helps us ground. If you have knee issues, you can put a blanket under the knees for padding.

- ⮎ Take the knees as wide apart as the mat and sit back on your heels. Rest the forehead down on the mat, or on a block if your head doesn't touch the floor. Breathe in and out several times, connecting the breath to the creative flow of the water element. Imagine the breath like waves in the ocean moving in and out of the shore of the physical body.
- ⮎ Walk your hands over to the left side, resting your chest on the left thigh and stretching longer through the right side of the body. Stay here for five breaths. Then walk the hands all the way over to the right side, stretching the left side of the body for five breaths.

- Come back to the center for another five breaths, making an intention to connect to the creative flowing energy of your breath and body through the practice.

- Come up to hands and knees and then stretch back to Downward-Facing Dog. Stay in Downward Dog for several breaths, sensing the energy in your arms, hands and legs.

- Walk your feet slowly up toward your hands and hang in a loose forward bend, with bent knees, either letting your hands fall to the floor or holding opposite elbows.

- After five or six slow, deep breaths, roll up to standing.

Anjaneyasana: Crescent Lunge: This pose is part of the Chandra Namaskar Sequence, Moon Salutations, which we'll do next. Holding the pose provides stability and strength in the pelvis as well as a deep stretch for the psoas and hip flexor of the back leg and the outer hip of the front leg. Releasing this tension and increasing mobility in the pelvis increases our capacity to receive the energy of creation and utilize it. You can modify the pose by keeping your fingertips on the floor or on blocks. You can also place padding under the back knee.

- From Tadasana (Mountain Pose), fold forward and place your hands on the mat on either side of your feet. Step your left foot back to a lunge. Keep your right knee over your ankle as you stretch your left knee back and down to the floor. Point your left toes.
- Allow your right knee to move three inches forward to align over the center of your right foot as you press down firmly into your right toes and heel.
- Stretch your arms overhead and interlace all your fingers except the first fingers and thumbs to create "steeple mudra."
- Draw your outer left hip forward and your outer right hip back. Lengthen your tailbone down as you lift the abdomen in and up.

- Move the pelvis forward and stretch the sides of your waist upward.
- Begin to arch your upper back slightly and squeeze your arms into your ears to support your neck as you look up toward your hands.
- Hold the pose for eight breaths, feeling the balance between strength and flexibility in your pelvis, while creating a powerful flow of energy that moves through your body.
- When you finish, release your hands down to the mat. Tuck your left toes under, lifting your knee, and step your left foot forward. Then step your right foot back to repeat the pose on the other side.
- Imagine your body like a crescent moon in the sky, illuminating the darkness with its soft glow.

Chandra Namaskar: Moon Salutes: This sequence of movements is designed to warm up the whole body in a nonaggressive way, focusing on opening the hips and flowing from one movement to the next the way water flows downstream. *Chandra* means "moon." The lunar element connects us to our shadow and our feminine energy.

- Begin in Tadasana (Mountain Pose). Take three deep breaths in and out, letting the breath energy move through your body. Breathe in light, breathe out darkness.

◐ Inhaling, reach your arms overhead, touching your palms together.

◐ Exhaling, fold forward, placing hands or fingers on the floor.

➲ Inhaling, lift your chest, bringing your fingers to your shins.

➲ Exhaling, step your left foot back to a lunge. Bring your left
knee to the floor gently as you did in Anjaneyasana (Crescent
Lunge).

➲ Inhaling, hook your thumbs and reach your arms overhead.

➲ Exhaling, release your hands down and step back to Downward-Facing Dog.

➲ Inhaling, roll forward to Plank Pose, bringing your shoulders over your wrists. Engage your abdominal muscles and quadriceps.

➲ Exhaling, lower your knees and then your abdomen and chest to the floor.

➲ Inhaling, slide forward along the earth like a snake until the front of your body is flat on the floor. Then place your hands by your low ribs with bent elbows and flat palms. Roll your shoulders back, lifting your head and chest off the floor into Bhujangasana (Cobra Pose). In this pose, your body looks like a snake lifting its head.

➲ Exhaling, press into your hands, lift your hips and stretch back to Balasana (Child's Pose).

➲ Inhaling, come up to hands and knees.

➲ Exhaling, stretch back to Adho Mukha Svanasana (Downward-Facing Dog).

➲ Inhaling, reach your right leg straight back, keeping your hips level.

➲ Exhaling, step your right foot up between your hands and bring your left knee to the floor again.

- Inhaling, hook your thumbs and stretch your arms overhead, spreading your fingers wide as you straighten your arms.
- Exhaling, bring your fingertips back to the floor and tuck the back toes under, lifting your back knee.

- Inhaling, step your left foot forward, lengthening your spine.

➲ Exhaling, fold over your legs.
➲ Inhaling, reach your arms up overhead touching your palms.

➲ Exhaling, bring your hands to your heart.

⮑ Repeat the sequence on the left side, and then repeat the entire sequence, both right and left sides, twice more for a total of six times.

⮑ Once you have the sequence memorized, you can focus on the flow of your breath and on the energy moving through your body.

⮑ When you finish, come to stand at the front of your mat in Tadasana (Mountain Pose) with your hands in prayer position in front of your heart. Pause for a few moments and feel the vibrant fluid energy coursing through your body. The more you can connect the physical experience to your conscious awareness, the more powerful it will be.

Malasana: Garland Pose: This pose is a deep hip-opening posture. It's the position used in many Eastern countries for doing work, birthing babies and evacuating the bladder and bowels. It cultivates *apana* (downward-flowing energy), helping us to release the darkness that holds us back and step into the light.

- From Tadasana (Mountain Pose), inhale as you reach your arms up overhead. Exhale to fold forward over your legs. Separate your legs a bit wider than your hips and turn your toes slightly outward.

- Bend your knees, coming down as far as you can into a squatting position. If your ankles are tight, you may find it helpful to place a rolled blanket under your heels. If you have a knee or hip injury, you can sit on a step stool or a yoga block to support your weight.

- Align each kneecap with the second and third toes of that foot to protect the knee joint.

- As you sit deep into your hips, slide your elbows to the inside of your knees and press your palms together in prayer pose. Press your elbows into your knees as you pull the prayer palms down toward the bottom of your chest.

- ⊃ Lift your chest and broaden your collarbones.
- ⊃ Stay here for eight to ten breaths, closing your eyes and focusing on letting go of the darkness that holds you back from stepping into your light.

Lizard Pose: This pose provides a deeper version of Anjaneyasana (Crescent Lunge). After Malasana (Garland Pose), it is easier to deepen this pose. This posture is great for people with tight outer hips and inner thighs, but can be destabilizing for people who are quite flexible in the pelvic area. Remember that while we want to deepen our flexibility, we also want to create more stability through our practice. If you have naturally loose joints, consider propping your elbows up on blocks and engaging your pelvic-floor muscles in this pose.

- ⊃ From Malasana (Garland Pose), place your hands on the floor inside your feet directly beneath your shoulders and step your left foot back into a lunge.
- ⊃ Turn your right toes and knee slightly outward and allow your left knee to come down to the floor.
- ⊃ You can do this pose with straight arms, keeping your hands on the floor or coming down onto your forearms to deepen the stretch. If your elbows don't quite reach the floor, you can place your forearms on blocks.

- Keep hugging the right thigh in toward your right shoulder to create more stability in the pelvis and knee. Let your back thigh melt toward the floor.

- Allow your neck to relax, releasing your head toward your hands, and close your eyes. Your hands can be in prayer pose or your palms can be facing up.

- As you take eight deep breaths in and out, observe the spaciousness from the left inner knee to the right inner knee opening you up from the inside out. Notice the stability from the right outer hip to the left outer hip providing you with structure and support.

- When you finish eight breaths on the right side, lift your chest and straighten your arms, tuck your back toes under again and step your left foot forward. Then step your right foot back and repeat on the other side.

- Incorporate the mantra "I allow both pleasure and pain to move through my body." (This mantra was extremely useful to me in labor, during which I incorporated both Malasana (Garland Pose) and Lizard Pose.

Eka Pada Kapotasana: One-Legged Pigeon Pose: Pigeon Pose is an intense stretch for the outer hip and glute. The intensity comes from stretching these large tense layers of muscle in the body and from becoming more receptive when we're used to activating these muscles to create power. Pigeon Pose teaches us to surrender to what *is* so that we become part of that natural flow of creative life-force energy that connects all living things.

- ➲ After Lizard Pose, walk back to Downward-Facing Dog.
- ➲ Stretch your right leg straight back as you inhale. Then exhale, sliding your right knee forward to the back of your right wrist. Place your knee on the floor behind your right wrist.
- ➲ Point your right toes toward your left hip, creating a diagonal angle with your right shin.
- ➲ Keep your left toes tucked under as you wiggle the ball of the left foot back a few inches to get your pelvis closer to the floor. Keep your hips centered. Don't let your pelvis roll to the right side. This may feel easier, but it will create a misalignment in the hips and knees.
- ➲ Place the left kneecap on the floor and untuck your left toes. Then walk your hands forward, coming down onto your forearms. Place your forehead on a block or bring your forehead all the way to the floor.
- ➲ Hold the pose for ten to twenty breaths. This will give you the opportunity to experience the quality of surrender that makes this pose so beneficial. Close your eyes and repeat the mantra "Let go" on the inhale and 'Letting go' on the exhale. "Let go' inhale, 'Letting go" exhale. This will help you relax and release into the pose to receive its nurturing benefits.
- ➲ When you finish the right side, press into your hands to lift your chest and step back to Adho Mukha Svanasana (Downward-Facing Dog). Pause for a few breaths, noticing the spaciousness in your right hip before taking the pose on the left side. Repeat the mantra on the left side.

Once you finish this short practice, you can lie down in Savasana (Corpse Pose) for several minutes and/or come into a seated meditation. Your hips will be nice and open for sitting comfortably. I suggest doing this sequence when you're feeling tense, when your creativity seems to be stagnating or when you're running from your shadow side. Doing these poses mindfully will help you release tension while bringing you back into the natural flow of life. They will also help you learn how to embrace your shadow side.

Body/Mind Reconditioning Exercise: The Wave of Change

Most of what we experience in working with pain and pleasure is in the mind. We think certain experiences will bring us pleasure and others will bring us pain. We may hold in our minds the idea that a hot cup of coffee is the only thing that will bring us pleasure first thing in the morning and that exercising will only cause us pain. The Wave of Change is designed to help us replace the connections we've made with the pleasure of something we want to let go of and the pain of something we want to embrace.

For example, if you really want to get in shape but every time you think of working out an image of a screaming trainer beating you with sticks comes to mind, you probably won't make it a priority. However, if when you think of working out you see yourself glowing with sweat and looking happy and fit, with toned muscles and loads of energy, you'll be much more likely to want to go to the gym. The following exercise can help you change any association you hold in your mind. You can turn the association you have between cigarettes and pleasure to one of extreme disgust. Or you can turn the association you have between doing your taxes and being completely overwhelmed to being confident and productive.

Bring to mind an image of yourself behaving in a way that you no longer want to behave. What is that behavior for you? Is it overeating sugary foods, getting frustrated in traffic, fighting with your partner? The image should be of you right before you're about to do that thing that you no longer want to do. Close your eyes. See yourself right before you're about to say that thing, eat that thing or think those thoughts. Now create a big screen in your mind and place this image in bright color on the screen.

- Create an image of you as the person who behaves the way you want to behave—the person who has fully released this behavior. For example, if you're letting go of eating sugar, the image of you might have really healthy teeth, more energy, a trimmer waistline and the look of satisfaction. What does the you who's free of the sugar-eating pattern look like, feel like, act like? Now put this image—small and in black and white—at the bottom left corner of the big color image of you about to do the old behavior.

- Look at the old pattern for a moment and then watch the small pattern in the bottom left corner swing up and crash through the big image of the old behavior. Make the image of the new you bigger and brighter. See the version of you that's free from that habit. Repeat this five times fast, clapping your hands as the new you breaks through the old habit.

- Check and see how you feel about the old habit or pattern. If you're still pulled by it, come back to the new version of you. Imagine in more detail who you are and what your life looks like. What else happens in your life as a result of letting go of this thing that isn't serving you? What are you stepping into that *is* serving you?

- Come back to the old picture in your mind and swing the new picture up through it, clapping your hands as the new picture takes its place. Do this five more times fast.

- Once more, imagine yourself as the new version of you. Feel the way you feel when that habit is no longer even an option and the new way of being feels like who you really are. Make that image bigger and brighter and play one of your favorite songs in the background. Smile to yourself. Take a deep breath in and out and then wrap your hands together and squeeze to imprint that new version of you into your body. Breathe that in and out a few times and then let it go and open your eyes.

Any time you want to reconnect to the feeling of yourself as the fit, healthy nonsmoker or the calm, patient parent—whatever it is that you chose to embed in your mind and body—all you have to do is wrap your hands together and squeeze. This will send the message to your mind and body to *be* the version of you that embodies this new habit. If you find yourself slipping into the old pattern, just redo the whole exercise a few times. It takes only a few minutes of reconditioning and a clear intention to make profound changes in our behavior.

The Union of Opposites

Pain and pleasure, shadow and light are two sides of the same whole. The tension created is the creative energy from which new life springs. It's the energy that fuels great art of all kinds—music, painting, dance, photography, sculpture, poetry. When we're able to overcome our fear of our own shadow, when we're able to embrace our own light, when we allow ourselves to experience both pleasure and pain fully, we can transform into the dynamic beings we're born to be.

Ask yourself these questions:

- How does this tension fuel my creative energy?
- How can I embrace the opposites in my life?
- What might this allow me to do or see?

The Hindu religion deifies Shiva, the still point of consciousness, and Shakti, the energy that tirelessly dances around it. You can't have one without the other. Each one of us embodies both the still point and the dancer within us. When we allow them both to arise, we can experience the fullness of who we're meant to be.

CHAPTER 4

Moving from Fearful
to Fearless

"There are two basic motivating forces: fear and love. When we are afraid, we pull back from life. When we are in love, we open to all that life has to offer with passion, excitement, and acceptance. We need to learn to love ourselves first, in all our glory and our imperfections. If we cannot love ourselves, we cannot fully open to our ability to love others or our potential to create. Evolution and all hopes for a better world rest in the fearlessness and openhearted vision of people who embrace life."
— John Lennon, *In His Own Write*

Fear is sometimes defined as "False Evidence Appearing Real." We look to the past or we make up something about the future to corroborate the feelings of resistance and anxiety within us. When we're afraid, we perceive our situation not as it is but as we *expect* it to be.

Fears often arise due to what the Yoga Sutras call *samskaras*, imprints in the mind that cause us to continue repeating habitual thought patterns and behaviors. We all have *samskaras*. Some of them are useful, like the *samskara* that helps us perform our morning routine. But many are not, like the one that causes us to cringe when the phone rings and we see a certain person's name appear on the screen. These imprints keep us from experiencing the freshness and possibilities of the present moment.

When my dog Rosie was a puppy, one of my friends came over to visit, and in an attempt to be playful, he stomped in slowly and growled her name, "R-o-o-s-i-e-e." She looked up at him in terror and immediately peed on the floor near the front door. Realizing he'd frightened her, he cuddled her and even gave her a treat, but for several years after that, every time any man came to the door, she automatically peed on the floor. That one incident shaped her entire perception of men. I tried many things to get her to stop, like shutting her in the bedroom until the man was fully in the house, or holding her when I answered the door (which resulted in getting peed on). Eventually, when my husband, who was still my boyfriend at the time, started spending most of his time at my place, we had to get serious about retraining her. We hired a dog trainer who sent Nick in and out of the front door about a dozen times in a row, and that's what finally worked. The continual coming in and going back out broke the association in her brain between a man coming into the apartment and the fear that caused her to pee on the floor.

Hopefully, most of us have learned to work with fear to the degree that we can control our bladders, but we all have fears that cause us to behave in ways that are less resourceful than we'd prefer. The Body/Mind Reconditioning exercises in this chapter will teach you how to unlink your mind from these recurring fears and create a new link in your mind to something neutral or even pleasant.

How Fear Limits Us

"Life shrinks or expands in proportion to one's courage." — Anaïs Nin, *Mirages: The Unexpurgated Diary of Anaïs Nin, 1939-1947*

Fear can stop us from doing the things we want to do, from loving and opening our hearts to others and from making changes in our lives that would be for our highest good. When we're frightened, the body responds by creating the fight-or-flight response. To produce this response, the hypothalamus in the brain activates the sympathetic nervous system through nerve pathways and activates the adrenal-cortical system through the bloodstream. This causes the body systems to speed up, and we become highly alert and tense. Our pupils dilate, our heart beats faster to pump blood to the extremities and our digestion shuts down, as it's not essential in that moment. This is useful if we're running across the street to avoid oncoming traffic but not so helpful if we're about to make a presentation to our boss and co-workers. Also, if we don't expel this energy by running from or physically fighting with the perceived threat, lactic acid builds up in our muscles, making them stiff. Then we store the cortical hormone in our bodies as chronic stress.

This is the root cause for most disease in the body—spending too much time in fight-or-flight mode and too little time in rest-and-digest mode. If you've ever seen a gazelle on a nature show, they don't spend the entire day worried about lions attacking. They go about their business of finding food and water and resting. They go into fight-or-flight only when the actual lion appears. But how many of us hold the image of our own lion in our minds from the moment we wake up in the morning until we exhaust ourselves at night?

When we don't address our chronic fears, they turn into phobias. Phobias can send us into full fight-or-flight mode when we just think of the thing that scares us. One of my friends was so afraid of heights that when we went on a hike in Colorado, she made it about a hundred yards onto the mildly inclining path before turning back. "I'm good," she said. "I'll be at the car." Despite the dozens of people safely making their way along the path, her nervous system told her she was in danger and sent her into flight mode.

A similar thing happened to me when I went scuba diving. We had an hour-long crash course in a swimming pool before heading out into open waters off the Australian coast with our instructor. I thought that because I practiced yoga, deep breathing and meditation every day, I'd have no problem relying on an underwater breathing apparatus and a person I'd never met to keep me alive. However, after descending about fifteen feet below the surface, I panicked. Images of my big brother dunking me under water when I was a child filled my mind.

Until that moment, I'd forgotten that I don't even like to have someone press on my shoulders in a swimming pool, much less take me to the depths of the ocean. I looked at my instructor and pointed vigorously upward. He seemed to be trying to persuade me to stay down, but I wasn't interested. He'd told us to move to the surface slowly to avoid a rapid change in pressure, but I couldn't. To his chagrin, I shot up to the surface like a cork shooting out of a Champagne bottle and practically leaped into the boat. I spent the rest of the afternoon floating above water, where I felt safe. I regret letting fear get the best of me, but I learned a valuable lesson about the power that fear can have over our rational minds.

The Yoga Sutras say one of the greatest obstacles to our enlightenment is *abhinivesha*, or clinging to life out of fear of death. Patanjali, the author of the Yoga Sutras, notes that fear of death stalks even the wise. When we're intensely afraid, we often feel as if we're dying, making it impossible to access our rational minds and make wise decisions.

How We Work with Our Fears

"Tell your heart that the fear of suffering is worse than the suffering itself. And that no heart has ever suffered when it goes in search of its dreams, because every second of the search is a second's encounter with God and with eternity." — Paulo Coelho, *The Alchemist*

"No heart has ever suffered when it goes in search of its dreams," He writes. Coelho doesn't say no *being* or *mind* has ever suffered in such circumstances. The mind may in fact suffer when we go in search of something beyond our fears, because it will be asked to surrender its strong hold on us to something yet unknown. If only we could remember that the heart is so nourished by stepping beyond our fears that even the sense of dying, which the mind finds terrifying, may to the heart be experienced as a sense of falling into the arms of divinity.

The mind, however, can be very stubborn. We need to employ practical approaches to help us work through our fears. The simplest one is to dialogue with the mind. When fear arises within you, try asking the part of you that's frightened the following questions (it can be helpful to use a journal to maintain clarity between the part of you that's frightened and the part that's curious):

- What do you think is going to happen if I (insert the thing you're afraid of)?
- What are you trying to protect me from?
- What do you really need in order to feel safe?
- How can I best support this need as I let go of the fear?

A slightly more complex approach is a Body/Mind Reconditioning exercise to address intense fears that may have turned into phobias. One of my yoga teaching apprentices admitted that she almost canceled her second public yoga class because she was so nervous about getting up in front of a group of people to teach. She found it very confusing because at her corporate job she had no problem speaking in front of her co-workers about pie charts and graphs, projected earnings and the like. But when she started talking about breathing, moving the body and feeling into the heart, she went into an altered state of panic.

After asking her more questions about this fear, she remembered a time in elementary school when her teacher asked the class who could spell *handkerchief.* Her hand shot up, and the teacher called on her.

"H-A-N-K-E-R-C-H-I-E-F," she said confidently.

"No! You are wrong," the teacher said.

While many adults (including me) probably would have spelled that word incorrectly as well, something about having been so certain and then being told she was wrong shattered her confidence. She was somehow able to regain it in her corporate job by focusing on facts and making sure she didn't make mistakes, but in the less concrete world of yoga and mindfulness, she couldn't rely on her facts to keep her safe.

I guided her through the phobia release process a week before she taught the final class required for graduation from yoga teacher training. And while she says she was still quite nervous, she didn't let it stop her from teaching, and the nervous energy didn't keep her from sharing something authentic with the group.

Body/Mind Reconditioning Exercise: Phobia/Fear Relief

You can do this process on your own or have someone guide you through it. I recommend doing it a few times over the course of a week so you can approach it from different states of mind.

Answer the following questions aloud if you're working with someone or write them in your journal if you're working alone:

- What is your phobia or fear?
- Can you think of a specific time you first felt the fear or the strongest recurring experience of the fear?
- What images come up when you think of the fear: sounds, feelings, sensations?
- Quickly draw an image that represents the fear.
- On a scale of one to ten, write down how strong the fear is for you.
- Do you want to let go of this fear?
- What would be the positive consequences for you of letting go?
- What are the negative consequences of holding on to this fear?
- What is your present state of mind about the fear right now?
- How would you like to feel about it? State only in the positive. For example, if you're afraid of cats, you wouldn't say, "I want to not be afraid of cats." You'd say, "I want to feel comfortable in the presence of cats."

Once you've answered these questions, begin the visualization process that follows.

- Count backward slowly from ten to one as you imagine walking down steps into a theater and choosing a seat in front of a big blank screen.
- Imagine a scene of the phobia playing on the screen, and then float up out of your seat so high that the screen becomes a tiny dot. See how insignificant it is in relation to your vast awareness. Then slowly float back down again into your seat.
- Play the scene in black and white with no sound, like an old silent film.
- Speed it up, playing it forward first and then backward.
- Add bright colors and humorous music, and fast-forward and rewind a few more times.
- Give everyone in the film a funny costume and wigs. Keep the humorous music and the colors. Play forward and back at high speed several times.
- See the screen go blank and notice how you feel.
- Place a new image of yourself on the screen—calm, relaxed and free of fear.
- If you notice any fear left in your body, play the scene one more time at high speed while moving your legs fast like you're riding a bicycle.
- Come back to the calm image of yourself. See your face relaxed, your body at ease. Watch your chest rise and fall with slow deep breaths until the image gradually fades to black.
- After a few moments, slowly walk out of the theater feeling calm and relaxed. Count from one to ten as you walk back up the staircase. Then step back into your body in the room.
- Notice how strong the fear is now on a scale from one to ten? If it's above a five, do the process again.
- Now, even if your fear level is zero, draw a *new* image of the thing you were afraid of and include yourself in the image.

When you've finished the process, sit for a few moments feeling the calm energy that's replaced the fear. You might try doing this process a few days in a row to get the most benefit. We often think of our fear as a monolith, impossible to move, but it takes only a shift in perspective to move from fear to equanimity, the place in which we have the most access to our genuine selves.

Yoga to Strengthen Our Bodies and Challenge Our Fears

In a recent Total Transformation Workshop, to challenge our fears we worked through a sequence that included Adho Mukha Vrksasana (Handstand). This pose can elicit fear in many people, especially those who haven't been upside down in many years. People often find excuses for not trying the pose. *My arms are too weak. My shoulders are too tight.* I won't allow these excuses to stop people from attempting the pose. I give them a strap to place around their upper arms or I stand behind them and hold their hips and say, "Now try again."

I noticed a woman in the class pretending to try, hoping I wouldn't see her, but given the topic of working with fear, I was on the lookout. I walked over to her and asked if she wanted a little help getting upside down. "My hamstrings are too tight," she said. "No, it's your mind strings that are too tight," I replied. She laughed and agreed to try. As it turned out, her hamstrings *were* tight, but all she needed to do was bend her knees. With a little help levering her legs overhead, she found her handstand and held it for at least five seconds. When she came back down, she was elated. She'd chosen to let her heart soar even when her mind protested.

The following poses will help to strengthen and tone the core as you challenge your fears. On a physical level, this sequence helps us establish stability in our lower backs to cultivate balance in the more challenging poses. On an energetic level, we're stimulating the third chakra, Manipura, which is located in the solar plexus, the area of the body below the ribs and above the navel. Manipura is the energy center related to our fear and self-doubt as well as our personal power. If Handstand isn't something you've done regularly on your own against the wall, I recommend saving it until you're in the company of a qualified teacher.

Abdominal Sequence: This sequence is designed to begin heating up the core body and bring a strong awareness to the actual location of the core, the muscles located around the abdomen, lower back, middle back and sides of the body. This is also the area of the body where Manipura resides. The sequence can be done one to three times. If you're pregnant, you should save this sequence for four to six weeks after you give birth. If you have a hernia or lower back pain, rather than attempting this sequence on your own, it's best to work with a qualified teacher so he or she can observe you and make adjustments as needed.

- Lie on your back with your knees bent and your feet lifted so that your shins are parallel to the floor and in line with your knees. You can modify by placing your feet on a wall.
- Place your hands behind your head, interlacing your fingers and keeping your elbows wide, in line with your shoulders.

- Take a deep breath in, and as you breathe out, lift your head to contract your abdominal muscles.
- Hold for five deep breaths, training yourself to breathe as you engage the abdominals. Exhale as you lower down and then release.

- Extend your legs straight up, bringing the toes directly above the hips. It's okay to bend the knees a bit if the hamstrings are tight.
- Keeping your hands behind your head, take a deep breath in, and as you exhale lift your head up again.
- Hold for five deep breaths, possibly lifting and lowering the hips an inch in unison with each breath. Note that this isn't a rocking-back-and-forth motion but an up-and-down motion to work the lowest abdominal muscles.
- Take a moment to lower your head and bend your knees.

- ➲ Extend the legs again and lower the right leg halfway down as you lift your head in your hands. Hold for five deep breaths. Then switch legs. Lift the right leg up and lower the left leg halfway down for five breaths.

- ➲ Lift both legs and lower your head. Draw your knees to your chest and relax with your breath. Feel the heat you've quickly created in the belly and let it energize and fuel you throughout the day like the warmth of the morning sun.

- ➲ As you become stronger, you can repeat this sequence one or two more times.

Ardha Chaturanga Dandasana: Plank Pose: Plank Pose offers a superb way to integrate the abdominal strength you've developed in a way that will help you do more complex poses like Handstand with greater stability and ease. Often, people who do lots of abdominal exercises still have poor posture and trouble activating those muscles in a way that helps them do anything other than the abdominal exercises themselves.

- ⮩ From your hands and knees, align your shoulders directly above your wrists. Spread your fingers wide and press down into your hands.
- ⮩ Lift the spine up slightly between the shoulder blades and gently draw the abdominal muscles in and up.
- ⮩ Stretch one leg back and then the other, tucking your toes under and lifting your heels up.
- ⮩ Lift your thighs to hip height as you press down into your hands and fingers.
- ⮩ Lengthen the crown of your head forward, gazing out on the floor in front of your fingers as you hold the pose for five slow, deep breaths.

- ⊃ When you finish, bring your knees to the floor and rest in Child's Pose or just press your hips up and back to Downward-Facing Dog if that's a comfortable pose for you.
- ⊃ Repeat Plank Pose three times, working on extending the number of breaths you can stay in the pose. One of my clients in her mid-seventies can hold Plank Pose for several minutes! She's my inspiration every time I feel like coming out of the pose early.

Adho Mukha Svanasana: Downward-Facing Dog: This pose is included in the first sequence as a way to ground physically and mentally. In this sequence, it's included as a way to prepare the body for L-Shaped Handstand, which is essentially the same shape as Downward-Facing Dog, with the feet on the wall rather than the floor. Downward-Facing Dog is also a great pose for stretching the hamstrings in preparation for Handstand. Be sure to focus on pressing your hands into the earth as a way to strengthen the upper body and prepare for going upside down.

- If you're in Child's Pose, lift up to Plank Pose and then bend your knees slightly and shift your hips back and up as far as you can without moving your hands or feet.
- Spread your fingers wide, turning your fingers slightly outward. Press each finger down equally into the earth.
- Fully straighten your arms and draw your hips away from your head.
- Our intention in this pose is to lengthen the spine. If you fully straighten your legs, you may start rounding your lower back, which is counterproductive. Focus more on lifting the hips up and back rather than reaching the heels down.
- Allow your neck to relax, but keep working your upper arms to support your shoulders. Strong straight arms in this pose will help you go upside down more easily.
- Spread your toes and point your heels back, directly behind your ankles.
- Hold the pose for eight breaths. Breathe slowly and deeply, feeling the strength in your arms increasing with each breath.
- Walk your feet up to your hands. Fold forward for a few breaths before rising up to standing to prepare for the next pose.

Virabhadrasana 3: Warrior 3: This challenging pose has taught me that it's okay to keep practicing a posture I may never master, because in doing so I master something else, the art of persistence. Through persistence we grow stronger in our bodies and minds. Virabhadrasana 3 (Warrior 3) is the most strengthening and, I think, the most challenging standing pose to do correctly. You must engage your arms, legs, back and abdominals and maintain your balance in order to hold the pose. The pose can be modified with a bent standing knee or by keeping your arms by your sides. You can also do this pose with your hands on the wall if you're working therapeutically.

- ⊃ From standing in Tadasana (Mountain Pose), place your hands on your hips, bend your knees and step your left foot back into High Lunge.
- ⊃ For High Lunge, align your right (front) knee directly over your right ankle and stretch your left leg back, balancing on the ball of your left (back) foot.
- ⊃ Align your shoulders directly over your hips as you reach your arms overhead, keeping the arms straight.

- ⊃ Take a deep breath in as you lean your torso forward. Breathe out as you reach out through both arms and lift your left (back) foot and leg off the ground.

- ⊃ You can reach your arms forward for more of a challenge to the upper body or draw the arms alongside your waist for a less intense variation.

- ⊃ Roll your inner left (back) thigh and heel up as you lift the whole left leg parallel to your torso.

- ⊃ Pull your outer right (standing) hip back even if you need to bend your right knee to keep the hips level. This is what makes the pose so challenging. It's best to keep a "micro-bend" in your right (standing) knee to avoid straining the knee or the hip.

- ⊃ Align your body parallel to the floor and ceiling from your fingertips or the crown of the head (depending on your arm position) to your left heel.

- ⊃ Hold the pose for five breaths, gazing down at the floor without dropping your head.

- ⊃ To come out of the pose, bring your hands to your hips. Then bend your right (standing) knee and come back to High Lunge by placing the ball of the left foot back down.

- ⊃ From High Lunge, lower your hands to the floor. Then step your back foot forward and rest in Standing Forward Bend. (See description of Standing Forward Bend below.) Then repeat the pose on the other side.

Uttanasana: Intense Deliberate Stretch or Standing Forward Bend:
This pose is an excellent pose for stretching the hamstrings. It's also a
good resting pose after Warrior 3 or Handstand.

- Stand with your feet together or hip-distance apart.
- Fold forward over your legs, resting your hands on the floor
  or on blocks. If your back or hamstrings feel tight, it's best to
  bend your knees to create less strain as you stretch the back of
  your body.
- Stay here for several breaths between the two sides of Warrior
  3 and use this pose as a resting position before coming into the
  following posture.

L-Shaped Handstand: This pose helps build confidence as well as strength in the arms, shoulders, core and legs in preparation for Handstand. To be safe, practice this pose with a skilled teacher the first few times. You need to be able to easily hold Plank Pose for several breaths and do Downward-Facing Dog comfortably to do this pose safely. When you're ready, you'll feel the inner confidence and strength it takes to go upside down and support your own weight with your hands. If you're pregnant, you can do this pose with supervision.

- Start by placing your mat perpendicular to the wall with the short edge touching the wall.
- Sit facing the wall with your legs straight out in front of you and reach your arms overhead. Flex your wrists as if pressing your hands into the ceiling and press your feet into the wall. This is the shape you'll make when you go upside down.

- ➲ Turn around, placing your hands where your hips were. Come onto your hands and knees, keeping your hands the same distance from the wall, which is the length of your legs.

- ➲ Come into Adho Mukha Svanasana (Downward-Facing Dog) with your heels against the wall, making sure your arms are firm and straight. Your stance will be shorter than your regular Downward Dog.

- ➲ Look between your legs as you step your right foot up onto the wall, level with your hips. Press the foot firmly into the wall.

- ➲ Step your left foot up onto the wall. Press the foot firmly into the wall, keeping your feet hip-distance apart.

- ➲ Straighten your legs while keeping your arms straight, making sure your hips are directly above your wrists and your heels are in line with your hips on the wall. You have now turned the 'L shape" upside down.

- ➲ Look at your hands and breathe while keeping your abdominal muscles engaged.

- ➲ Hold the pose for five to ten breaths, invoking all the fiery energy you've accumulated by facing your fears. Breathe slowly and deeply.

- ➲ Step one foot back down to the floor at a time. Shift forward slightly and rest in Balasana (Child's Pose) again for about one minute.

- ➲ Feel free to do the pose again if you have the energy. If not, practice the pose daily to build strength. Eventually, you'll be able to safely do a handstand. If you already practice Handstand, this preparation pose will make your handstand sturdier, safer and more precise.

Adho Mukha Vrksasana: Handstand: The literal translation of the name of this pose is "Downward-Facing Tree Pose." In this pose, we pull up the roots of our feet and legs, which we so comfortably keep on the earth, and turn them upside down, changing our entire relationship with gravity. We face our fear of being out of control and change our perspective, which helps us get unstuck from our limited view of the world. As mentioned earlier, if this pose is new to you, it's best to do it with a qualified teacher, but if you've been working on it in class for a while without success, this may be the time to try it on your own.

- ➲ Come into Downward-Facing Dog facing the wall, with your hands shoulder-distance apart and your fingertips three inches from the wall.
- ➲ Shift your shoulders over your wrists into Plank Pose, making sure your head doesn't hit the wall.

- ⮑ Step your right foot halfway to your hands while lifting the left leg straight back behind you. Just like in Warrior 3, keep the hips level, lifting the inner thigh of the back leg up.

- ⮑ Bend your right knee and push off the floor, levering the lifted leg into the air.

- ⮑ Keep your hips square with your shoulders and keep your arms straight. Look forward between your hands as you kick up.

- ⮑ If this doesn't work, try the other leg. It's best to do the pose twice, working with both legs to create a balance of strength and flexibility between the right and left sides.

- ⮑ When you do get upside down, straighten your arms even more. Press down into your hands and draw up through your waist and hips. Flex your feet and reach your heels up the wall vigorously.

- ⮑ When you become very comfortable here, try drawing one foot and then the other away from the wall to challenge your balance.

- ⮑ When you're ready to come down, lower one leg at a time in order to move more slowly.

- ⮑ Rest in Child's Pose for several breaths before you try again.

Transforming Limiting Beliefs into Empowering Beliefs

"It's not who you are that holds you back—it's who you think you are not." — Attributed to Hanoch McCarty, co-author of *Chicken Soup for the Soul*

We all have certain beliefs that place limitations on our potential. Think of humans, who once believed that the world was flat and that if you sailed too far, you'd simply fall off the edge into an abyss. It took almost five hundred years for the majority of people to shift that belief. Almost five hundred years for people to understand that the world is in fact spherical and that we can travel all the way around it, attracted toward its center by gravity. Changing this limiting belief to a more empowering one was a huge step in human thought.

Now think of all the beliefs you hold in your own life that keep your world flat when in fact your world is round and so much bigger than the horizons you can currently see. Do you tell yourself you aren't good enough at something to pursue it as your work? Do you tell yourself you won't be able to feed your family if you take a job that feeds your soul? Do you tell yourself you're not the right age, height, weight or color to do what you want to do, have what you want to have or be what you want to be?

We all do this. It's a way of keeping our world flat and small so that we don't have to challenge ourselves and possibly fail in the process. But as they say, if you never try, you've already failed.

One of my clients went to an arts college and dreamed of being a landscape architect. But the family business was real estate finance, and as the youngest of four children, he felt enormous pressure to do as the other three had done. So every morning he put on a suit and went to the office, following in the footsteps of his father and brothers. He wanted to please his father and he liked what he did. He was also grateful that this career afforded his own family a very comfortable lifestyle, but it didn't feed his soul. In his subconscious mind, he held a belief that if he did what he truly wanted, he wouldn't have the approval or the support he needed.

Thirty years later during a shamanic journey, we brought this limiting belief into the light. He believed that at this point in his career, there was no way he could change jobs. I suggested that rather than quit his job, he simply get a sketch pad and some colored pencils so he could do a little drawing at his desk between phone calls and meetings.

For several weeks I asked him every time we met if he'd gotten the pad and pencils yet, and every time he had an excuse for not doing it. But the real reason was that he'd cut himself off from the artist inside him. He'd allowed his limiting belief to sink so deep inside him that he couldn't even buy a pad and pencils for doodling at his desk. We've all done things like this. The longer we resist something, the more power we give to that resistance. Then it often feels like it's too overwhelming to take even a small step toward change. I have a friend who's never been out of the state where she was born. Although she dreams of going to the beach, it seems like an impossibility because somewhere along the way she told herself she couldn't do it.

Eventually, after taking several healing journeys and consciously changing his limiting belief to an empowering one, my client was able to start drawing. It brought up a lot of hidden emotions and desires that he'd pushed down, such as the desire to travel to the Southwest and draw the landscapes. He's still working on integrating this belief into his conscious mind, but through these practices he's already made a huge shift. Through persistence and conscious awareness, his world has turned from flat to spherical and hasn't fallen apart as he feared it would if he put down the phone and picked up his pencils.

Body/Mind Reconditioning Exercise: Transforming Our Beliefs

As the McCarty quote suggests, it's our beliefs about who we *are not* that limit us. Be honest when exploring the following questions, but also be gentle with yourself. After a lifetime of believing something, it may take a little while to shift to a new perspective. I suggest you write down the answers to these questions in a journal or notebook.

- What are your limiting beliefs about yourself in relation to your body?
- What are your limiting beliefs about yourself in relationship to your work? (This can be your current job or related to changing your work, answering your calling.)
- What are your limiting beliefs about yourself in relationship to love, intimacy or friendship? (This can be related to a romantic partner or your friendships or family relationships)
- What are your limiting beliefs around finances, money, etc.?
- What other limiting beliefs do you hold about yourself, your life and your circumstances?

◔ Take a moment to read over your answers. Notice similarities in word choice and in how you feel when you read them. Choose the three that have the most energy for you.

◔ Replace each of the limiting beliefs with new empowering beliefs. Make sure the new beliefs are stated fully in the positive and in the present. For example, I wouldn't say, "I am not a loser." I would say, "I am a winner." And I wouldn't say, "I will make more money at my job." I would say, "I am experiencing great financial abundance."

◔ Speak your new empowering beliefs aloud. You can do this in front of the mirror or with a friend over the phone. You can speak them out to your cat or dog or baby. Who else hears you matters less than that you hear yourself.

◔ Notice how it feels in your body to say these things aloud. Try standing up tall, with good posture. You can even dress up in a way that helps you to better embody this belief. Kids do this all the time in order to feel that they're truly embodying whatever it is they want to be that day. My son often wears a red cape around the house before school and asks me to play his favorite songs as he gets pumped for the day. If your new belief is, "I am a successful businesswoman," put on a suit and some heels. Stand in front of the mirror and say this to yourself as many times as needed for you to start believing it. If your belief is "I am athletic and fit," put on your running shoes and gym clothes and do a few push-ups or jog in place before you say your new belief. Trust me, your dog won't be fazed by your new behavior. And since you already have your shoes on, you might as well run or walk around the block a few times to get started!

◔ Write these new empowering beliefs in bold, bright colors on clean white paper and hang them up somewhere that you'll see them every day. I challenge you to say them aloud for no less than seven days in a row. Thirty days is even better.

Once you've truly begun to embody these new beliefs, your life will organize itself around them. It can't be any other way. I used to hold the belief that I was someone with a weak immune system. I told myself lots of stories about why this was true, and each time I got sick I'd say, "Look, I told you so, universe. I'm just a sick person." But when I realized that at the very least, my beliefs weren't helping me stay healthy, I did this exercise. Then every time I felt a twinge of sickness or even fatigue, I'd say to myself, "I am strong and healthy. The well-being of the universe is flowing through me, nourishing my body and mind." I said it several times and did my best to *feel* it as I said it. It took a little while to master, but now I say it in my mind even if I hear someone else on the train cough or sneeze. I say it to them in my mind: "You are strong and healthy. The well-being of the universe is flowing through you, nourishing your body and mind." That isn't to say you'll never again get sick, but I can tell you that changing your limiting beliefs to empowering ones dramatically increases the likelihood of changing your life and health for the better.

Shamanic Journey to the Underworld

Journeying is said to be the meditation of the shamans. In order to journey, shamans put themselves into a slightly altered state, just as Buddhist meditation masters do. My teacher calls this place "infinity," where time and space become irrelevant. For me it's much like the dream space. Have you ever noticed that when you're dreaming, you can be anywhere at any age? You can meet anyone from your past, people you haven't seen for twenty years, even people who have passed away. In your dreams, you can fly or you can simply arrive in one place and then the next without having to travel through time and space to get there.

Journeying is conscious dreaming. When we journey to the underworld, we're looking into our past to find the old memories or imprints that formed our limiting beliefs. As the Yoga Sutras say, *samskaras* can be active or latent. We may have a latent memory from early childhood that's still dictating our behavior today. Shamans, Buddhists and yogis believe that these imprints can come from this lifetime or from one of our many past lives. Many of us repeat the same patterns lifetime after lifetime until we learn how to change them. Journeying is an excellent way to learn how to make these changes.

Some traditions believe that journeying for yourself is ineffective because your mind will block out what it doesn't want to see, just as it does in everyday life. I've found that when we surrender to the process, just as we must surrender our thoughts in meditation, we can access far more than we ever imagined. That said, if you've experienced an intense trauma such as sexual violence or war that you haven't worked through with a qualified counselor, it's best to do the journey with a skilled shaman who will go on the journey on your behalf.

Whether I'm guiding a group to journey for themselves or going on a journey for an individual client, I always remind them that we aren't going into the underworld to bring these painful memories and imprints back so that we can live them out again. We're simply recognizing that they're there so we can let them go and free ourselves to step into our new empowered selves.

I suggest reading through the following process a few times before attempting it on your own. When I lead a group, I use a drum or a rattle to create a rhythm for the journey. You can also play soft rhythmic drumming music to help regulate your breathing and quiet your thinking mind as you journey on your own. I love the track "Shamanic Journey," by Anugama. Finally, remember that you're in charge. If you're not ready to see something, if you're not ready to let something go, just move on. The spirit that guides us is benevolent. It will never force us to go somewhere we aren't ready to go.

- Look back at your list of limiting beliefs. Notice which one holds the most negative energy for you. Then make an intention to journey in order to see the origin of this belief and let it go.
- Lie on your back in a comfortable position. I recommend lying on the floor rather than in your bed so that you don't fall asleep.
- Close your eyes and begin breathing in through your nose for five counts and out through your mouth for five counts. You can increase this number as much as is comfortable for you. Slow deep breathing helps calm the nervous system and quiet

the thinking mind. Imagine the breath as a circle. Connect the inhale to the exhale and the exhale to the inhale. Visualize the breath energy as a circle of light moving from your pubic bone up the front of the body to the crown, down the spine to the tailbone and back up the front of the body. After ten to twenty rounds of breathing, check in. If your mind is still agitated, do ten more. Otherwise you can begin the journey.

- See your energy body slowly standing up and walking to a door. Outside the door are a field and a hole. Let yourself slide down into this hole the way you slid down the tube slides on the playground as a child. Feel the cool damp earth on your skin as you slide down, down deep underground.

- At the end of the hole, you land in a pool of water. On the other side of the pool, you see a waterfall. Walk over to the waterfall and stand under it, allowing the water to pour over your body, cleansing you to your very soul.

- When you feel ready, swim to the edge of the pool and stand on dry ground. Here you see a forest and an opening to a path in the foliage. Walk along this path through the thick forest until you come to a clearing. In the clearing, you see a large smooth stone. Sit on the stone and look around you. Notice the trees and the sounds. Notice any animals that are present. Know that you are perfectly safe.

- When you're ready, walk to the edge of the clearing, where you will see another path. This short path will lead you to a cave. There will be a stone blocking the entrance to the cave. Inside the cave is the memory that will teach you what you need to know about this limiting belief.

- Push the stone to the side. If you think you can't do this, ask yourself, "What am I resisting? What do I not want to see? What would happen if I let myself see this?" These answers may help you remove the stone, but if not, don't force it—just come back to the clearing and sit in meditation for a while, getting to know the terrain of the underworld.

- If the stone moves to the side, step in and have a look. Notice what you see without any judgment. Don't try to figure out what it means—just look around. If someone is inside, ask what is happening. They may tell you exactly what the memory is. For example, they may say, "I'm getting in trouble for lying," or, "I'm drowning." Don't try to help them. Remember they are just memories. Instead, ask them, "What do I need to learn from you?" Or, "What do you want me to know?"

- They will tell you something such as, "Mommy only loves me when I am well-behaved." When you hear something like this, you know it's the root of your limiting belief. Even if what they say sounds totally out of sync, just listen—don't try to change it or help them.

- Once you have your answer, close the cave and go back to your stone. Sitting on the stone, ask yourself, "How has this imprint affected me? Am I ready to let it go?" If the answer is "no," that's okay. Sometimes the first journey is about just seeing what's present. If the answer is "yes," walk back to the cave, roll away the stone and blow white light into the cave with the intention of sending that heavy energy back to the light of the divine. See that image losing its charge and dissolving into white light. When you finish, close the cave again and walk back to the stone in the clearing.

- Sit here for a moment and ask the forest if any power animals want to come back with you. An animal may emerge quickly or slowly. If it does, ask it to come into your body through the solar plexus, the third chakra, so that it may help empower you. Feel the animal's strengths and attributes helping you to step into your new beliefs.

- When you're finished, stand up and walk back through the forest to the pool of water. Standing perfectly still, look down into the pool and see an image of yourself reflected back to you. Look closely—this is your true self, the you that was present before you were born, the you that will be present after you die. Know that this reflection of you is perfectly healed and whole.

Draw this reflection of you into your heart chakra, allowing it to spread down to the root and up to the crown, enveloping your whole being.

- When you're finished, lie down in the pool and allow the gravity of your physical form to call you back. When you reach the opening in the earth, let it draw you up and up, back to the surface of the earth.

- Walk back through the door and lie down in your physical body. Take a few moments to allow your energy body to settle into your physical form. When you're ready, roll to one side and sit up.

When you finish the journey, take a moment to write down anything that felt important to you. Then look back at the limiting belief you chose to work with and the empowering belief you transformed it into. Does the wording and essence of this new belief still feel like what you want to embody? If you need to change anything to make the belief even more potent, do that. Then go to an actual mirror and see yourself embodying that new belief. You may even see some slight similarities in your appearance to the power animal that chose you. It was said that the great saint Neem Karoli Baba could shape-shift from human to monkey and back again before the eyes of his disciples. When we fully embrace a power animal, we become one with it. When we fully embrace a new belief, it becomes a significant part of who we are.

If you're interested in learning more about shamanic journey work, I suggest reading Alberto Villoldo's book *Mending the Past and Healing the Future with Soul Retrieval* as well as Sandra Ingerman's *Shamanic Journeying: A Beginner's Guide*.

Fear as a Message

"I learned that courage was not the absence of fear, but the triumph over it. The brave man is not he who does not feel afraid, but he who conquers that fear." – Nelson Mandela, anti-apartheid activist and Nobel Peace Prize winner

Ultimately, fear is a signal. In some cases it's a signal of danger that we should avoid, but in many cases it's a signal that we're coming up against one of our self-imposed limitations. When we recognize a self-imposed limitation, we choose whether to back away or break through. The more we do something, the better we get at it. So if we back away when fear arises, we'll get better at backing away until our lives become very small. If instead we break through, not only does it become easier to do the next time, but our world also expands to a new self-created border.

In the incredible book and film *Room* (spoiler alert: I'll be giving the plot away), a young woman who was kidnapped at seventeen has a child while in captivity. For the first five years of her son's life, he knows nothing of the outside world. Much like the belief that the world was flat, he thinks that everything on TV is actually inside the TV and that there is nothing beyond the room they live in but the bit of blue sky he can see through the skylight overhead. After his fifth birthday, his mother decides he's old enough to learn the truth about the world outside the room.

Even as a child skilled in imagination, it takes him a while to believe what his mother tells him. Part of him finds her explanation of the world too big and scary to believe in. But through her insistence, he starts to understand. When the time comes for him to make a daring escape by playing dead until he reaches the outside world, he's terrified, but he does it anyway. Maybe he does it because his mother tells him to, or maybe it's for the same reason we all risk the unknown: for the chance to expand our experience of who we are.

Due to his bravery, he escapes, his mother is found and freed and their captor is sent to prison. Afterward, they both go through a difficult time of readjustment in the outside world. When the boy suggests they go back to see the room, his mother is tentative, but because he trusted her, she trusts him. When they do go back, he realizes how small and confining that space was and how much he's grown since leaving. Think what would have happened if his mother had been too scared to let him escape? Think what would have happened if he'd been too scared to try?

We can all draw inspiration from this young boy. I challenge you to risk leaving the confines of what's safe and known, especially if it's painful. I dare you to stretch your wings and fly into the ever-expanding vastness of who you are and to never let the limitations of your mind hamper your infinite heart.

CHAPTER 5

Expanding the Heart

"When we let go of our battles and open our heart
to things as they are, then we come to rest in the
present moment. This is the beginning and the end
of spiritual practice. Only in this moment can we
discover that which is timeless. Only here can we
find the love that we seek. Love in the past is simply
memory, and love in the future is fantasy. Only
in the reality of the present can we love, can we
awaken, can we find peace and understanding and
connection with ourselves and the world."
— Jack Kornfield, *A Path with Heart:
A Guide Through the Perils and
Promises of Spiritual Life*

The physical heart is not only a vital organ but a masterpiece created by
the universal intelligence. Its four chambers work nonstop throughout
our entire life, pumping oxygen-rich blood to our bodies and removing
oxygen-poor blood. When our heart functions optimally, all the other
systems and organs in the body are able to perform their functions with
greater ease and efficiency. When there's a problem with the heart, such as
a blockage in one of the passageways, problems arise for the whole body.

The same is true of the energetic heart. The energetic heart houses Anahata, the fourth chakra, which is the intersection between the denser physical aspects of our being and the subtler mental aspects of self. When our energetic heart is pumping out good feelings and removing bad feelings from our energy body, the heart chakra functions optimally and causes us to feel happy, peaceful, loving and kind. When Anahata is blocked, we don't receive as much good energy as we need and we begin to experience more negative feelings, such as sadness, depression, anger and fear.

As humans, we tend to suppress our emotions in order to stay within the confines of acceptable behavior. This often leads to stagnation in the heart until eventually something dislodges those pent-up emotions and everything comes spilling out. The term "going postal" comes to mind. If you've ever visited a post office in New York City and seen the long lines of disgruntled people waiting for their packages face off against the mostly apathetic postal workers stationed behind thick glass, you can imagine that eventually someone on one side of that glass is going to completely lose their mind.

Several years ago, Australia revamped its postal system. It got rid of the glass windows and dreary lighting. It started selling greeting cards, office supplies and colored markers. It trained its employees to be friendly and helpful rather than fearful and apathetic. The effect is astonishing. Not only are the employees happy, but so are most of the customers. When I lived in Australia, I found myself looking forward to trips to the post office rather than dreading them.

Our hearts are like this. We may subconsciously believe that if the bulletproof glass is thick enough, we'll be protected from emotional pain, when in truth this protection actually blocks the flow of good feelings from coming to us and prevents the release of bad feelings from within.

When we put down the armor, invest in some genuine greetings and allow ourselves to display our true colors, we give others permission to do the same. Then we can begin to connect on the level of the heart, as was intended by its creator.

In the Buddhist tradition, the spiritual heart consists of four abodes, or chambers: loving-kindness, compassion, sympathetic joy and equanimity. I find it interesting that the word *abode*, which refers to the spiritual heart, means home or living space, and the word *chamber*, which refers to the physical heart, means essentially the same thing. Just like the physical heart becomes stronger through exercise, the spiritual heart grows more robust through practice.

Loving-kindness means being friendly to oneself and others, wishing one another well and acknowledging our interconnectedness. Compassion means acknowledging the pain and suffering we all experience and doing what we can to ease that suffering for ourselves and others. Sympathetic joy means being genuinely happy for others, understanding that when we celebrate the victories and joys of others, we experience them as our own. Equanimity means maintaining internal balance in the face of external imbalance. It's recognizing that what happens to us and around us need not determine our own inner experience.

A saint from India once explained to his disciples that when he's alone, his mind rests in equanimity. When his friends or students visit, he naturally calls on what is needed in the moment: compassion for the suffering, joy for the thriving and kindness to everyone. This sounds like a pretty amazing way to go through life.

Most of us can't say the same. We spend so much time in the mind that even when we're alone we don't experience equanimity. The other day I spent the entire thirty minutes of my meditation writing an e-mail response in my mind to a friend who had slighted me. Looking back, it's clear that I wasted that precious time. Had I been able to remember that experiencing equanimity is a choice in any situation, I could have traded my mental machinations in for trust, trust that everything is unfolding just as it should, trust that if I cultivate evenness in my heart, the things that happen around me won't change who I am.

Sometimes I remember this and sometimes I don't. The key to this practice is to surround ourselves with as many reminders as possible, so that little by little our lives begin to look like the Indian saint's. We begin to rest in equanimity in traffic and send compassion to the stressed-out drivers around us. We begin to rest in equanimity at our child's sporting event and offer sympathetic joy to the other team when they win. We begin to rest in equanimity at a party where we don't know anyone except the host and begin to treat all the "strangers" with kindness until everyone feels like a friend.

What Does It Mean to Open the Heart?

In the yoga world, the idea of "opening the heart" has become cliché. One of my more cynical teacher friends once said, "If it was as easy as doing backbends and chest-opening stretches, every gymnast and contortionist would have an open heart." She was right. As much as we yogis would like to believe that doing a backbending practice will make us more compassionate and kind, it's not quite true. I do, however, believe that the body, mind and energetic heart are intimately connected, and opening the physical home of the heart (the chest and upper back) is a good place to begin this work of opening the energetic heart.

Walking down a crowded street in Manhattan, I observe many people with shoulders slumped, heads down and faces frowning as they look at their phones or their feet. I'm sure they've seen me doing the same thing from time to time. This physical posture is the first obstacle to creating an open heart.

When students arrive in the yoga room at six fifteen on a weeknight still holding this posture (some still holding their phones), I have them lie back with a yoga block between their shoulder blades and a folded blanket under their heads. I encourage them to close their eyes, relax their shoulders and open their chests. When they do this, they begin to breathe. They begin to soften and let go of the bulletproof glass they've been hiding behind throughout the day. I find that after being given permission to rest for a few minutes, students are more likely to try new poses, to let go of self-judgment and to lighten up a little.

During a recent healing session, one of my regular students told me that when she attends a super-vigorous yoga class, she can barely make it to Savasana. She spends the whole class huffing, puffing and trying to keep up with the gymnastic students half her age crowded around her. On the other hand, when she lets herself off the hook and comes to my Level 1 class, she feels good about herself and carries the feeling with her for a little while afterward.

To me, this is how we should feel after taking a yoga class. Life is so often competitive and serious. We feel pressure to perform at work, in our relationships, in our friendships. Yoga can be either an extension of that pressure or an antidote. As far as I'm concerned, the most advanced students in class are the ones who will move their mats over when someone comes in late, the ones who giggle when they fall out of a balance pose, the ones who take Child's Pose when they're weary and the ones who can lie in Savasana at the end and truly relax. When someone is able to do these things, they are much more able to do what is required to open the heart.

What Causes the Heart to Close?

Loving-kindness, compassion, sympathetic joy and equanimity are wonderful qualities, but they're not easy to maintain and summon at will. All of us have experienced the pain of rejection at some point when we've opened our hearts to another human. When I was three years old I had an overwhelming urge to run up to every child in the grocery store or on the playground and hug them tightly. This unabashed affection usually resulted in fear and crying on the part of the other child. Attempting to protect me from rejection, my mother tried to explain that you can't just run up to strangers and hug them. "It scares them," she said. I remember being very sad about this. I don't remember consciously choosing to stop, but I do know that a fear of initiating hugs and staying in an embrace for too long stayed with me for many years to come.

When I take my son to school in the morning, his best friend runs to him with open arms ready to hug. My son is more like one of those kids I frightened. "Not yet," he says to his friend. "I'm not ready." It's so tempting for me to force him to hug his friend, but I know that this will backfire later. When I pick him up from school in the afternoon, he has warmed up and gives a hug to everyone who wants one on his way out.

The thing I couldn't understand when I was three is that opening our hearts doesn't have to be an invasion of someone's personal space. It doesn't even need to be reciprocated by another person for us to receive the full benefits. Ram Dass talks about experiencing the opening of his own heart with the bank teller and the grocery clerk. He says that as he was beginning to love people, he didn't know what to do about it. Then he realized that there is actually nothing you have to *do*. *Being* a loving presence is the key. And from that place, we can act with an open heart when we're called upon to act.

When my college boyfriend broke up with me, I felt like my heart was actually breaking into pieces. I'd thought he was the one I would be with forever. I couldn't imagine myself without him. I felt alone and confused, and to top it off, my parents, who had been married for almost thirty years, had recently announced they were getting divorced. I cried every day. There was nothing for me to hold on to. The only thing I knew to do was run. I began training for a marathon and cried my way through miles and miles of training. Eventually, the tears stopped coming. I got stronger and started running farther and faster. My mind became clearer, and I started to see a tiny glimpse of the possibilities available beyond my last relationship and even beyond my parents' marriage. This was when I first recognized the true resilience of the heart. No emotion is actually strong enough to stop the heart from beating, and it's only strong enough to stop the heart from loving if we choose to let it.

Rather than shutting down, I opened up. I raised money with a friend for a homeless shelter for pregnant women. I started doing yoga and meditating. I studied my butt off and got great grades during my senior year. And at my graduation party, my ex-boyfriend showed up and told me he regretted breaking up with me.

My best friend (after having had a few beers) waved her finger at him. "You snooze you lose, buddy! You snooze you lose!"

I admit it felt good to hear that he wanted me back, but as I looked around at my great friends and my new boyfriend, I realized that I didn't need him like I'd once thought. I was happier and more empowered without him than I had been when we were together, and it was time for us both to move on.

Opening the heart is not just about recovering from the loss of romantic love. It can be about recovering from the rejection of a parent, a teacher, a friend or a situation. My mother has told me that when she was five years old, she climbed up into her stepfather's lap hoping for some affection and he told her to get off of him. It wasn't that she was unlovable or even that he didn't love her. He just didn't have the capacity in his own heart to make that much space for her. But as a child, all she "knew" was that someone who was supposed to love her didn't.

When I recently took my children to visit my mother's stepdad, whom I consider my grandfather, he referred to our new baby as "it." He admitted that babies scare him, because he doesn't want to hurt them. I can imagine that this fear is what caused him to push my mother away. He also claims to hate dogs, yet my grandparents have had one or more dogs for at least the past forty years.

As it turned out, over several decades of caring for his own children, grandchildren and great-grandchildren, he'd softened up a bit. When I came into the living room, where he still sits in the same chair he's sat in since I was a child, I found my son sitting on his lap and my dog curled up at his feet. Sure, he looked a little uncomfortable, but he didn't push my son away.

"You know that dog of yours is really good," he said. This is the same dog he rejected when my aunt presented her as a gift at his fiftieth wedding anniversary, which is why I had her in the first place. Over the course of his long life, he'd learned to do what was hard for him. He'd learned that this is how you love people.

Parents and teachers have bad days. Friends can hurt us when *they're* hurting. Lovers will leave us for a million different reasons. This is why it's so important for us to focus on loving ourselves. Another cliché we've all heard is that we must love ourselves first. This adage is often misinterpreted as selfishness or narcissism. Loving ourselves first doesn't mean that we always do for ourselves first, that we take the best for ourselves and leave the remnants for others. It means we recognize that the wellspring of love we seek isn't coming from outside. It's bubbling up from within. We're like fish in a vast ocean asking everyone where the water is when, as it turns out, it's everywhere. Just as love is everywhere that we choose to see it.

When we're able to truly love ourselves, we're practicing unconditional love—we know everything about ourselves and we choose love anyway. We know that we stole a bottle of vodka from the liquor store at sixteen, that we have to shave our big toes every morning to prevent stubble and that we didn't make it to the hospital in time for our grandfather's passing because we were too scared. If we believe in a higher power, we assume that this higher power knows everything about us, too, and chooses to love us regardless of our actions.

"All you need is already within you, only you must approach your self with reverence and love," Indian saint Nisargadatta Maharaj said. "Self-condemnation and self-distrust are grievous errors. Your constant flight from pain and search for pleasure is a sign of love you bear for your self. All I plead with you is this: make love of your self perfect."

How Do We Learn to Love Ourselves?

If we can make love of ourselves perfect, we'll have no problem opening our hearts to others. *Perfect* in this case doesn't mean we have to love perfectly or be perfect. He's using the word to illustrate the importance of this practice. He's saying we must love ourselves completely, not leaving anything out, not even the greediness we hide from others or the fear we try to ignore. By *perfect*, he means "completely." We can start the process by tending to and releasing our old wounds.

Self-Compassion

On a five-day silent retreat in New England, Sarah Powers led us through a guided meditative practice designed to communicate with our wounded inner child. I remember how frightened I was when I looked in and saw this little girl, her long blond hair and gangly limbs all crumpled and crouched inside me, completely drenched in thick black tar, shaking, cowering and peering up at me. *Oh my God!* I thought. *Is this what I've been carrying inside me? It's a wonder I can function at all.*

When the initial shock of seeing her wore off, I was able to approach her. We were instructed to ask the child what he or she needed. In my mind, I said, *Hi, sweet one, you seem quite frightened. What is it that you need?*

She looked up at me with her big blue eyes untainted by the thick tar. *I need to be taken care of. I need to be loved.* She paused and looked down and started to whimper.

Okay, I said. *I'm right here. I want to take care of you and love you, exactly the way you need me to.* At first she stiffened against me, and then she relaxed, all gooey and tar-covered into my arms. In my mind, I smoothed back her hair so I could see her face and soothed her for a while. Then I imagined a bowl of warm water with frangipani flowers floating on it and I poured it over her head. She closed her eyes and let the water cleanse her. I did this several times until she was clean and free of the thick tar she'd been covered in. Then I swaddled her in a heavy pink towel that smelled of "April fresh" Downy the way my grandmother's towels smelled. I just held her in my arms until she fell asleep. It was one of the most transformative experiences of the heart that I have had.

A week or so after I returned home, my husband and I fought. But rather than punishing myself as I had done so many times in the past, I went into the bathroom, sat on the floor and closed my eyes so that I could see my little girl. I reminded her that I was there to take care of her and that even if she made a mistake, it was okay—that's how we learn. This is something my mother always told me, but what she didn't tell me and I can now give to my inner child and my own children is that we don't need to be punished for our mistakes. We simply need to learn to bring compassionate awareness to them.

Self-Forgiveness

I recently watched a television show about a group of kids who'd caused a car accident that landed all of them in juvenile detention for most of a year. It was the first time I'd seen so clearly how backward this system is, probably because it's easier to recognize the problem when kids are involved than when it's adults. Punishment doesn't cleanse the heart and help us become loving members of society. At best it makes us too fearful to commit crimes, and at worst it makes us resentful, vengeful and violent, increasing the likelihood that we'll offend again.

In Norway's Halden Prison, inmates are given good food, fresh coffee, private showers, flat-screen TVs and access to life coaching. The atmosphere isn't one of punishment but of rehabilitation. Halden's governor explains that the punishment his inmates receive is loss of freedom. He insists that the old model of making prison such a terrible place so that prisoners don't want to return doesn't work. People who are treated with respect and given the opportunity to change their lives while they're being detained have a far greater chance of actually doing so.

Halden is a new facility, so its success rates haven't been measured yet, but Norway in general has only 74.8 people imprisoned per 100,000 residents, compared with 236 inmates per 100,000 in the United States. And only 20 percent of those rehabilitated in Norway commit repeat offenses within two years, compared with 60 percent in the United States.

Buddhist nun Yin Kit, who runs a meditation program in Canadian prisons, insists that the inmates not come to class in shackles or chains. In an interview with the online blog, Buddhist Door Global, she said, "I think every time the handcuffs are put on, there is a drop in self-esteem and self-confidence, and also thinking that they are no good," she says. "These people have made mistakes. We have all made mistakes. Can we support them? This is what the practice is about—the whole practice of the Buddha's teaching—to be compassionate and to embrace each other's shortcomings."

Most of our mistakes don't land us in prison, but we often create a prison in our minds in which we punish ourselves over and over for a single offense. When we make a mistake, rather than berating ourselves, we can use the Norwegian model of rehabilitation and the Buddhist model of compassion. We can offer comfort and kindness to ourselves and treat ourselves with civility in the process of recognizing what we've done wrong and how we can do better in the future.

The next time you cause harm to yourself or someone else, try asking yourself these questions:

- What did I do that was not useful?
- How did I hurt someone else? How did I hurt myself?
- How could I do something different in the future to avoid causing suffering?
- Can I love and forgive myself in spite of this mistake?

These are useful questions that help us create loving change.

Opening Our Hearts to Others

The work of opening our hearts to others begins right where we live, with the people around us. When we can see them—their goodness and selfishness, their mistakes and triumphs—and allow them to see these things in us, without running away, we move further along the path to enlightenment than we could by sitting alone in a monastery. Unconditional love, which I learned first from my mother and father, is the work of the heart. It is the essence of God.

Neem Karoli Baba had a few simple but profound teachings that needed not be complex, because he embodied them so fully. The one I aspire to master in this lifetime is "Love everyone and tell the truth."

To love everyone *and* tell the truth gives us all permission to be and to unfold together. When we enter into the space shared by our human family, it's essential that we bring this simple teaching with us—love everyone and tell the truth. When the truth is infused with love and free of criticism, it's incapable of causing harm. It becomes a powerful elixir for the delusion that causes most of the suffering we experience in our relationships. The truth at its core is that we are all worthy of love in every single moment.

The Four Abodes of the Heart

Also known as the four immeasurables, the four abodes of the heart—equanimity, compassion, sympathetic joy and loving-kindness—are the keys to opening the heart. In his book *The Wise Heart*, Jack Kornfield writes, "When developed, these qualities help to balance one another. Because love, compassion and joy can lead to excessive attachment, they need to be balanced with equanimity. Because equanimity can lead to excessive detachment, it needs to be balanced with love, compassion and joy. Together they express optimal mental harmony."

Equanimity

Equanimity is the ground for the other three abodes. At its essence, equanimity is nonreactivity in the presence of all that is eternally changing. In one teaching story, the son of a Chinese farmer was riding the family horse through the countryside one day and got bucked off. He broke his leg and wasn't able to help with the duties of the farm. The farmer's neighbors lamented, "Oh, that is such bad luck. We are sorry," to which the farmer said, "Good luck, bad luck, who knows?" The next week, military officials came barreling through the countryside demanding that all able-bodied young men join the army. Due to his broken leg, the farmer's son was left behind. His neighbor stopped by to chat. "Oh, you are so lucky they didn't take your son," to which the farmer replied, "Good luck, bad luck, who knows?"

As the story plays out, we see that the outer circumstances are always vacillating between what most would consider good or bad, but the farmer, in his state of equanimity, sees through the drama. Knowing he cannot control the winds of change, he practices nonreactivity.

Nonreactivity doesn't mean we're cold and void of feeling. It means we're able to step back from the daily drama that sucks us into suffering and draws us out of peace. It's like standing on a mountaintop and watching a battle below. From the mountaintop it's easy to see that no one fighting this battle will win. The battle itself is the cause of suffering. When we put our weapons down and become present with the unfolding of life, we naturally become nonreactive and equanimous.

Meditation is a wonderful way to cultivate equanimity. When we sit quietly without an agenda and watch the breath come and go, we can observe through our thoughts that much of what we consider good and bad is just our opinion based on our habits and beliefs. When we initially practice meditation, it might go something like this: First we feel calm. Then our back starts to hurt. Then we smell fresh coffee, which is pleasant but makes us want some. Then we get angry with the person who made the coffee and distracted us. Then we feel bad about being angry. Then we remember a time when we were very calm and did not get angry. Then we notice our feet falling asleep and wonder how much longer we have to sit still. Then the timer goes off and we feel sad that we wasted the meditation in distraction.

If we practice long enough, we begin to catch the mind jumping from good to bad more quickly, and instead of indulging it, we bring the mind back to the neutrality of the breath. Over time, the mind settles into this calm state like a puppy that finally realizes that barking at the door isn't going to bring its owner home any sooner, so it lies down for a nap. Breath-centered meditation will be described in greater detail in Chapter 7. Until then, as you go through your day, notice the vacillations from good to bad that you feel. Notice how others respond to what they perceive as good and bad. See what it feels like to practice nonreactivity. You might find that much of what you think of as good and bad is simply the natural unfolding of life.

Compassion

Compassion allows us to acknowledge suffering—our own or the suffering of another—and offer the energy of relief. We often confuse sympathy with compassion. Feeling sorry for ourselves or someone else doesn't help. Taking pity doesn't transform the pain. In fact, it may worsen it. Compassion is the practice of recognizing suffering and consciously transforming it by offering whatever relief we can.

Compassion practice doesn't mean we have to give away all our possessions or feel the bad feelings that someone else is experiencing. We simply recognize and offer what support we can in that moment. I remember looking out my hotel window in Mumbai, India, and seeing the villages made of cardboard boxes, held up by cinder blocks and sheet metal roofs, with buckets for toilets and no running water, and thinking, *There's no way I can go out there. If I do, the suffering will be too much to bear and I'll break into a million pieces.* It took me two days to get up the courage to walk out of the hotel and onto the street.

Due to jet lag, I was up before dawn. Just outside my hotel, I saw children in tattered smocks, covered in dust, sleeping on cardboard beds next to their mothers. My eyes filled with tears. It didn't seem fair that human beings were forced to live in these conditions. I wanted to scoop up all the children and take them with me. But then I saw a little girl waking up and snuggling into her mother's arms. Her mother held her close, petting her hair and kissing her head, just like I do to with my son when he comes into my room at 5 a.m. wanting to snuggle. "Just like me," I whispered to myself as a reminder of the Tonglen practice of transforming suffering into relief.

We can't give every child enough money to buy shoes and school supplies. We can't send every man or woman in need of medical care to the doctor. We can, however, open our hearts rather than closing them. When we do this, we see that those who are suffering, no matter how different they may look on the surface, are just like us on the inside, just as fragile and resilient, just as worthy of and capable of experiencing love.

In these situations, I've found the practice of Tonglen to be of enormous benefit. In Tonglen, we first recognize the suffering of another. We may do this in the moment, as we're walking down the street in a developing country or through the kennels at the Humane Society. We then breathe in the suffering of those around us. We don't try to run from it or shield ourselves from it. We breathe it right into our center. Then we imagine the suffering being transformed into healing light within our hearts. When we consciously breathe out, we send that healing light to those who are suffering.

We can also do this with a friend who's suffering from illness or going through a difficult time with his or her spouse. Rather than automatically jumping in with home remedies or relationship advice, we can sit and be present. Hold space for them, breathe in the suffering they're experiencing, turn it into healing light and breathe it out as relief. I guarantee, even if the person doesn't consciously know what you're doing, they'll feel the calm, loving support you're offering on a deep level.

This practice is especially useful when someone is attempting to cause us harm. Once when I offered a homeless woman a bag of trail mix, rather than taking it or just saying no, she started screaming at me about how she needed money, not trail mix. As I had been consciously practicing compassion before I even offered her the trail mix, I continued to do so when she yelled at me. She didn't seem to notice, but compassion practice kept me calm so that I didn't yell back at her. When someone yells at us and tries to belittle or embarrass us, it serves us to remember that they're probably suffering. If they were feeling happy and peaceful, they wouldn't be causing harm. When we remember their suffering, we can offer them compassion. This keeps our power intact and defuses the energy of the situation far more effectively than arguing ever could. In war there are no winners, but in peace everyone wins.

Sympathetic Joy

Another of the four abodes is sympathetic joy. This means being happy for another person when they're happy or experiencing good fortune. This can be a difficult quality to cultivate, especially when things aren't going so great for us personally. If a friend calls to tell us they've received a promotion at work while we've been laid off for two months, it can be very difficult to genuinely feel happy for them. The fortune of another often shines a light on our own misfortune. Rather than celebrate with them, we may silently berate ourselves for not being able to find a good job. *If I were as smart as her, I'd have a great job, too. If only I had his great sense of humor.* When we think this way, we allow a friend's success to take us deeper into our own well of unworthiness.

Just after traveling through India and before moving into an ashram in San Francisco, I attended a yoga conference in Colorado. Needless to say, I was experiencing some serious transformation at the time. I was also not looking or feeling my best. My body felt heavy and bloated. And as luck would have it, the airline lost my suitcase, so I spent four days wearing the same gold T-shirt and white pants from the ashram in India over a pair of high-waist granny panties purchased at a local camping store.

For some reason, a gorgeous petite blonde with more energy than a Jack Russell terrier befriended me. While I was glad to have someone to talk to and eat meals with, her fabulous hair, positive attitude and extensive wardrobe were like subliminal messages to my psyche: *You're fat, you're ugly, you look ridiculous in that outfit. Just stay in your room and hide.*

But I couldn't stay in my room. Something more important than the way I looked compelled me to press on. Despite my feelings of self-doubt, every morning I walked five miles uphill, through the majesty of the Rockies to the conference site.

Thinking that Yin Yoga meant relaxing yoga, I unwittingly signed up for a workshop with Sarah Powers. Like my new friend, Powers was also blond and thin and gorgeous, but there was something about her that was different. Just her presence suggested that it was through a life of some hardship and much deep inquiry, not through her lucky breaks, that she had landed in this place.

The class was not relaxing. It was excruciating. It forced me to sit with all the places within myself that I'd been ignoring, namely the deep well of pain and insecurity that was now showing up in my body. I decided to listen to this teacher and to let go of my self-judgment for a little while. I told myself I could always pick it up again if I needed to.

When the class ended and my new friend arrived to meet me, I decided to practice being happy for her instead of jealous. When she told me about her new husband, I did my best to set aside feelings of inadequacy for being single and to instead focus on her, This wasn't easy or natural for me, but it helped me enjoy her more and get out of my head enough to appreciate that I was in one of the most majestic places on Earth sharing my favorite spiritual practice with the best teachers in the world.

Sympathetic joy is the practice of being happy for another person regardless of our personal situation. Rather than thinking about how we match up to our friend or co-worker, we think about how great it is for them to be experiencing such good fortune. In our minds, we envision them thoroughly enjoying their new relationship or their new position at work. When we do this, we actually begin to feel those good feelings within ourselves. Rather than closing off to them by going into jealousy and resentment, we open up to them and experience the success, abundance and joy as our own.

Sports fans are great examples of this practice. They're great at celebrating the success of their favorite team as if it were their own success. If you look on the field after an athlete has made a great play and then up in the stands, you'll see the same glowing smiles and high fives among the fans as you do among the players. I think this is one of the main reasons people love watching sports. Even nonathletes have a chance to feel the triumph and glory that the elite athletes feel when they win. Now, if we can get the athletes to extend this same sympathetic joy to the opposing team when they win, we might see some very impressive heart opening in the world of sports.

Facebook offers a great opportunity to practice sympathetic joy. When we scroll through our newsfeed and see photos of an old high school friend traveling the world or a best buddy from college sitting on the deck of his summer home with his gorgeous wife and kids, rather than feeling jealousy, we can feel joy. We can close our eyes for a moment and smile. In our minds we can say, *I am really happy for you. I am glad your life is so full of joy, adventure and abundance.* We can let those good feelings flood through our bodies, and when we open our eyes, we can hit the "like" button and write an encouraging comment. The more we do this, the more joyful and abundant we feel within ourselves. We begin to recognize our own successes and blessings more easily and feel those feelings more frequently. So in truth, cultivating joy for others is cultivating joy for ourselves.

Loving-kindness

Loving-kindness is another of the four abodes. We can think of it as the chamber that holds well wishes for ourselves and others and pumps them out through the bloodstream of life that connects us all. The experience of loving-kindness encompasses compassion, sympathetic joy *and* equanimity. As a practice it gives us a framework for cultivating good feelings toward all beings.

We approach this practice by first consciously opening our hearts to a being we love effortlessly and unconditionally. I encourage people to choose a baby or a pet, someone who hasn't had enough time on the planet to cause a lot of drama. Then in our minds we send well wishes to this being, such as *May you be happy and healthy.* Once we've tapped into that generosity of spirit, we direct the well wishes toward ourselves. After that we direct them toward a neutral person, such as the mail carrier or a local grocery clerk. Then we stretch to include a difficult person, and eventually we send well wishes to all beings everywhere. By saying the same phrases again and again, we train ourselves to be kind and loving to everyone—not just the puppies and babies but also the bad drivers and the people who answer their cell phones in the movie theater.

Formal Loving-kindness Practice:

In the formal practice, you send the same well wishes to your loved ones, to yourself, to neutral people, to difficult people and to all beings everywhere. Below, I offer the phrases I use when I do this practice. You can certainly develop your own phrases once you get a feel for the practice.

Begin by sitting in a comfortable seat, either cross-legged on the floor with a cushion under your buttocks or in a chair sitting upright. Take a few minutes to quiet down and connect to your breath. Then bring your attention to your heart. Imagine opening up the space of your heart and letting a soft green light settle in among the subtle hum of the sound *yam* in the background. "*Yam*" is the seed mantra of the heart chakra. It's said to resonate at the frequency of the emotional heart.

To begin the loving-kindness meditation, first bring to mind a person in your life whom you find easy to love. If no one comes to mind, try using an animal. It's the essence of that loving energy that we want to connect to. Place that being in the center of your heart and say the phrases below, either in your mind or aloud.

May you be protected and safe.
May you be content and pleased.
May your body be free from illness, pain and fatigue.
May your body be strong, healthy and comfortable.
May you be free from mental suffering.
May you be free from attachment and aversion.
May your life unfold with joy, abundance and ease.
May you be the direct witness of your own true perfection.
May you be at peace.

Observe how you feel after this. You may get a boost of energy or a warm feeling inside or nothing much depending on the day.

Now bring an image of yourself to mind and place that image—not in detail but in essence—in the center of your heart and repeat these phrases as many times as you need to in order to feel at peace within yourself:

May I be protected and safe.
May I be content and pleased.
May my body be free from illness, pain and fatigue.
May my body be strong, healthy and comfortable.
May I be free from mental suffering.
May I be free from attachment and aversion.
May my life unfold with joy, abundance and ease.
May I be the direct witness of my own true perfection.
May I be at peace.

When you finish, take a few deep breaths in and out and notice how you feel.

Now choose a neutral person—your neighbor, your grocery clerk, your barista, your bank teller—and place that person in the center of your heart. Reconnect to the soft green hue and the subtle hum of *yam* and repeat the phrases again:

May you be protected and safe.
May you be content and pleased.
May your body be free from illness, pain and fatigue.
May your body be strong, healthy and comfortable.
May you be free from mental suffering.
May you be free from attachment and aversion.
May your life unfold with joy, abundance and ease.
May you be the direct witness of your own true perfection.
May you be at peace.

Notice how you feel. There may be a sense of compassion toward that person you've never thought about much or a vague feeling of kindness arising. Or perhaps you feel disinterested about sending well wishes to this person. Just observe without judgment.

Now bring your attention to a difficult person in your life. If you're new to this practice or feeling quite upset with someone in particular, it's wise to choose someone who doesn't evoke too much strong emotion. You'll find that if you practice regularly, even if you never send loving-kindness to someone who's very difficult for you, your energy toward them will shift as a result of sending it to other people. Once you've chosen that person, bring them into your heart. It should be someone you feel comfortable enough with to place in your heart. If you don't, choose someone else. Then repeat the phrases:

May you be protected and safe.
May you be content and pleased.
May your body be free from illness, pain and fatigue.
May your body be strong, healthy and comfortable.
May you be free from mental suffering.
May you be free from attachment and aversion.
May your life unfold with joy, abundance and ease.
May you be the direct witness of your own true perfection.
May you be at peace.

Observe how you feel afterward. Perhaps a bit agitated or sad. Grief may arise or more anger. You can repeat this one as many times as you need to, but don't force yourself to feel better—just allow yourself to experience what's actually happening with consciousness.

Finally, bring your attention to a greater image of all beings everywhere. Not trying to individuate, perhaps imagining the planet or the solar system sitting in your green expansive heart and humming with the sound of *yam*, repeat these phrases:

May we all be protected and safe.
May we all be content and pleased.
May our bodies be free from illness, pain and fatigue.
May our bodies be strong, healthy and comfortable.
May our bodies be free from mental suffering.
May our bodies be free from attachment and aversion.

May our lives unfold with joy, abundance and ease.
May we be the direct witnesses of our own true perfection.
May we all be at peace.

One summer I decided to start a loving-kindness flash mob. And while it was more like a flash very small gathering, the four to eight people who joined me every Friday afternoon experienced profound heart opening. We met at twelve thirty on the steps across from Whole Foods in Union Square, which is one of the busiest places in Manhattan. As everyone rushed by, we sat motionless, gazing softly straight ahead, and offered well wishes to loved ones, neutral people, difficult people and all beings everywhere. Tourists took our photograph. Preteens tried to distract us with silly dance moves. Some people tried to get us to talk. Most just walked by as if we weren't there. Endless streams of humans, most caught in the whirling of their own minds, passed by like leaves floating down a river.

During one session, a drunk man to the left of us sang, "The sun'll come out tomorrow," over and over and horribly out of key. The Hare Krishnas to our right chanted, "Hare Krishna, Hare Krishna, Krishna, Krishna, Hare, Hare," equally off key. Somehow the dissonant tones melded into the high-decibel ambulance alarms and the *blip blip* of police sirens being used to push the traffic along all merged into one.

When we came to the part of the meditation in which we sent well wishes out to all beings everywhere, I could feel my heart expand to include the bustling crowds before us, the tone-deaf singer and the Krishna devotees, then all the people in the high-rise buildings surroundings us, then all of New York City. It kept expanding like a wave in all directions until I experienced that limitless quality Buddha spoke of. When we take the time to truly recognize that despite our differences we are all part of the organism of life, it becomes almost impossible to feel lonely and separated.

Yoga to Open the Heart

This sequence focuses on opening the chest and thoracic spine while strengthening the upper back and shoulders. This means doing backbends, which can be quite confronting. We're used to protecting our hearts, seeing what's in front of us and hiding from what's behind us. However, in this practice we'll cultivate what Buddhists call an undefended heart. When we let go of defensiveness, which ultimately drains our energy and weakens us both physically and emotionally, we free up our bodies, hearts and minds. In this freedom, we can open up to a deeper capacity for compassion, gentleness and patience, which are the true characteristics of a strong open heart.

Sphinx Pose: This pose opens the chest as it strengthens the upper back and upper arms. It's an active antidote for the slump shoulders we get from sitting at our computers much of the day. It's also a fantastic therapeutic pose for the lower back, as the gentle compression of the lumbar spine sends increased blood flow to those tissues.

- ↻ Lie on the floor facedown. Then prop yourself up, placing your elbows directly under your shoulders with your forearms, hands and fingers stretched forward so that you look like the Egyptian statue of the Sphinx. Make sure that your elbows aren't too far back by your sides. They can be slightly forward of the shoulders but not behind, as this will cause neck strain.

- ↻ Press down into your forearms and lift your chest. Roll your shoulders down your back and lift the top of your head. Then close your eyes.

- ↻ You can hold this pose for anywhere from ten to fifty breaths. A shorter hold will energize the body. A longer hold will give you the opportunity to deepen your breath and sense the subtler opening of the heart and the spinal pathway.

- ↻ Visualize the inhale expanding the heart space and the exhale sending healing light down the back body, filling the kidneys and lower back. Allow the light to open the energy pathways down the whole back of the body.

- ↻ When you finish, turn your elbows out and rest your forehead on your hands for five breaths, letting the lower back, shoulders and neck relax completely.

Cat/Cow Vinyasa: While the word *Vinyasa* means "to place in a special order," a generally accepted meaning of the word is "moving with the breath." The Cat/Cow Vinyasa is a simple way to warm up the muscles along the spine, as well as to open the chest and shoulders, while moving with the breath. We move the spine back and forth from the shape of a swaybacked cow to a scared cat in order to access the full range of spinal motion without putting weight on the vertebrae. Cat/Cow can be done by almost everyone and is especially useful to pregnant women who may need to omit weight-bearing Vinyasa movements.

- Come to all fours in a tabletop position.
- As you breathe in, tuck your toes under, relax your abdomen and move your chest forward and up to arch your back as you roll your shoulders back and down.
- As you breathe out, untuck your toes, curl your tailbone under and draw your chin toward your chest, rounding your back as you exhale.
- On the inhale, tuck the toes and arch your back. On the exhale, point the toes and round your back.
- Repeat this sequence about eight times, moving slowly with the breath. Let the breath begin to lead the movement. Allow your body to follow.
- Make sure you don't exaggerate the movements. If you tend to sway the low back naturally, engage the abdomen a little in the cow movement. If you tend to round your upper back and hunch your shoulders, try to take the cat movement more into your middle and lower back.

⊃ When you finish, rest in Child's Pose for a few breaths, noticing the openness of the energy pathway you created through your spine.

Anahatasana: Heart Chakra Pose: Anahatasana is the quintessential heart chakra pose. While stretching the shoulders and chest, it physically enlivens the vital center of the body: the heart and lungs. Energetically, it stimulates the expansion of the four abodes. For those with tight shoulders or a neck injury, place your forehead on a block.

⊃ Come back up to the tabletop position used for Cat/Cow. Keep the hips directly above the knees while you walk your hands forward until your forehead touches the floor. If it doesn't touch the floor easily, place a block under the forehead.

⊃ Straighten your arms, keeping them active to hold your body in place. After a few breaths, you may feel that you can go deeper into the pose. At that point, you can move the block out of the way or place your chin on the floor rather than your forehead.

⊃ As you hold the pose for fifteen breaths, keep pressing into your hands and fingers and firming your upper arms. Roll the outer upper arms down and the inner upper arms up.

⊃ Let your chest soften down toward the floor, relaxing the muscles of your upper back. Close your eyes and surrender to the pose.

‒ As you breathe in, imagine drawing heart energy in through your palms and up to the center of your upper back, the back of your heart. As you breathe out, imagine pouring fear, defensiveness and anger out of your heart and onto your mat. Let your mat soak it up like a sponge and dissolve it into pure energy.

‒ When you finish, come into Child's Pose and rest for several breaths.

Salabhasana: Locust Pose: This pose is a safe and simple way to strengthen the muscles of the back body, preparing them for deeper backbends, which will require the extra stability. This pose is great for people with lower back pain, as it strengthens the upper back muscles, taking the strain off the lower back. It's not appropriate for women more than twelve weeks pregnant, as it places too much pressure on the lower abdomen.

‒ From Child's Pose, shift forward and slowly lower down onto the front body.

‒ Extend your arms back by your sides. Press the tops of your feet down and lift your kneecaps to activate the legs.

‒ Begin to lift your forehead, chest and shoulders off the floor. Keep pressing your feet down and breathing as you lift the upper body and arms away from the floor.

- Hold the pose for five breaths, spinning your inner thighs up toward the ceiling. Then come down to rest for a few breaths.
- As you do the pose a second time, try clasping your hands behind your back. If your hands don't meet, you can hold on to a strap.
- Bring your hands as close together as possible before straightening your arms, being careful not to hyperextend your elbows.
- Lift your head, chest and shoulders away from the floor again. Then lift your knuckles away from your tailbone. Finally, you can lift your legs away from the floor, pointing your toes straight back and keeping the feet hip distance apart.
- Spin the inner thighs up and the tailbone down.
- When you finish, release your hands and place them under your forehead to rest.
- You can repeat this pose one to three times to develop strength in the back body and prepare for deeper backbends.

Ustrasana: Camel Pose: This is a beautiful backbend that appears to be simple, but doing it safely and effectively is challenging. If you have a neck injury or lower back pain, it's best to do this pose with the guidance of an experienced teacher. This pose is a great backbend for pregnant women without neck or lower back pain. The pose demonstrates a deeper expression of exposing the undefended heart from a strong, supported foundation.

- From prone position, press back up to tabletop position. Then come to a high kneeling position with hips and shoulders directly above the knees. You can place a blanket under your knees for more cushioning if you like.
- Tuck your toes under so that your heels are higher up.
- Place your hands in prayer position, with thumbs pressing just below the bottom of the breastbone.
- Begin to lift the breastbone, lift the front hip points and draw down through the tailbone as you arch your heart up over your shoulder blades.
- Keep moving your thighs forward as you lift your front hip points up. And lengthen the back of your neck as you start to gaze at the ceiling.
- Reach your fingertips to your heels as you keep your hips in line with your knees. It can be helpful to do this pose with your front hips pressing against the wall. If your hips move away from the wall, you know you're probably sinking into your lower back.
- Hold the pose for five deep breaths, shining the loving heart energy that you cultivated in Anahatasana out from the center of your chest like a spotlight with a soft green hue.
- Continue to lift the chest and ribs off the hips as you come back to an upright position. Then untuck your toes and sit back to your heels, resting with hands on the thighs in a neutral position.
- Do the pose one more time for five breaths, continuing to reach actively through the spine and breathing deeply.
- When you finish, sit in Vajrasana (sitting on the heels) and slide your hands over your knees, curling your chin to your chest to

reverse the curve of the spine. Hold this counterpose for five breaths.

➲ Then sit for a few breaths in a neutral position observing the effects of the backbends. Notice how you feel.

Ardha Matsyendrasana: Half-Seated Spinal Twist: This pose actually translates to mean "half lord of the fishes" because the shape of the pose looks like a fish jumping into the air and curling around itself. But we call it Half-Seated Spinal Twist because that describes what you're actually doing. This pose stretches the outer hip while twisting the spine. It's a good pose to do after Camel Pose to stabilize this hips and release tension from the neck and upper back. Pregnant women should twist away from the knee that's closest to the chest.

- From Vajrasana (sitting on the heels), sit to the left of your heels. Then swing the right foot around to the outside of the left knee, keeping your right knee close to the chest.
- Make sure you're seated evenly on both sitting bones, and if not, place a blanket under both sitting bones to create an even seat.
- Bring your right fingertips to the floor behind your back and stretch your left arm toward the ceiling. Take a deep breath in as you reach.
- As you exhale, wrap your left elbow around your right knee, maintaining the length of your spine and the openness of your chest.
- Turn your head to the right and twist a bit deeper with each breath while keeping both sitting bones on the ground.
- Hold the pose for eight breaths, allowing the spine to twist evenly from the tailbone to the top of the head.
- Release, feeling the lungs and chest open up again, allowing deeper breath and a more spacious heart. Repeat the pose on the other side.

When you finish this sequence, lie in Savasana (Corpse Pose), resting on your back and allowing the full effects of the pose to sink in to your body, mind and heart.

Deep Heart Breathing: After doing these heart-opening postures, it's the perfect time to practice deep heart breathing. Sit in a comfortable position, placing one hand on the heart and the other hand on top of it. Close your eyes and take in a slow, deep breath through your nose. Feel your lungs and chest expanding slowly. Imagine your heart expanding, too. At the top of the breath, hold it for a few moments, imagining the qualities of equanimity, compassion, loving-kindness and sympathetic joy expanding within your heart. Then slowly release the breath through the nose, sending these qualities out into the world. Do this for no fewer than ten breaths. As you work your way up to twenty, thirty or even fifty breaths you'll feel the euphoria that comes from truly connecting to your own vital life force and opening your heart.

Limitless Heart

"Do not worry if your harp breaks, thousands more will appear. We have fallen in the arms of love where all is music. If all the harps in the world were burned down, still inside the heart there will be hidden music playing. Do not worry if all the candles in the world flicker and die. We have the spark that starts the fire. The songs we sing are like foam on the surface of the sea of being while the precious gems lie deep beneath. But the tenderness in our songs is a reflection of what is hidden in the depths. Stop the flow of your words, open the window of your heart and let the spirit speak." – Rumi, *The Essential Rumi*, translated by Coleman Barks

When I first read this quote, I thought the word *harp* was *heart*. I like it both ways. The harp is said to be the instrument of angels, and the heart is the instrument we humans use to make the music of our lives. When we're brave enough to open our hearts, to love ourselves and to love one another, we open up to all the possibilities the universe has to offer. When we don't let the fear of being hurt or rejected stop us from expressing our feelings for another person, we find that the love we're hoping to feel is growing within us. When we're courageous enough to say, "I love you," and mean it, we give others permission to do the same. The four abodes of the heart, sometimes called the limitless ones, are never-ending. There's no limit to how much compassion, kindness, joy and equanimity we can generate if we're just willing to try.

CHAPTER 6

Expressing Our Truth

"I believe that unarmed truth and unconditional love will have the final word."
— Martin Luther King Jr.

While Ram Dass was in India with his guru, he went through a period of being very angry with everyone. He saw all the other devotees in the Ashram as fakes and phonies. During this time, his cherubic guru, Neem Karoli Baba, had been offering a simple teaching to his devotees: Love everyone *and* tell the truth. In several of his recorded talks, Ram Dass tells the story of his guru calling him to the front of the room. "Ram Dass, love everyone," he said. Then he called him forward again. "Tell the truth," he said this time. This pattern repeated several times, and Ram Dass nodded his head each time, thinking he understood. Then one day as the devotees went on a pilgrimage, Ram Dass got so angry with the others that he refused to ride the bus and proceeded to walk several miles on dusty roads in the hot Indian sun. When he finally arrived at the destination, everyone was relaxing and eating. One of the devotees offered him a plate of food, which he refused rudely.

His guru then called him over. "Ram Dass, is something wrong?" he asked (as if he didn't know).

"I hate all these people," Ram Dass confessed. He said he hated everyone, including himself.

"But I told you to love everyone," Guruji reminded him.

"But you said, 'Tell the truth,' " he said, his eyes filling with tears.

"I told you to love everyone *and* tell the truth." He conveyed this from a place of such deep love and truth that Ram Dass instantly understood, not in his head but in his heart. The way I understand this is, *Love is the only truth. Everything else is simply an opinion.*

The first two precepts of yoga as outlined in the Yoga Sutras are *ahimsa* (nonviolence) and *satya* (truth). (Many teachings extend *nonviolence* to mean friendliness or love.) These two precepts come first because without them we can't truly follow the path of yoga, which is the path to union with the divine. The divine is made of pure love and therefore pure truth.

This being said, like Ram Dass, we're human. So while we may wish to love everyone *and* tell the truth, our truth may not yet be in alignment with pure love. It might take time and practice with expressing what we think is our truth in order to peel back the layers of opinion, fear and defensiveness to get to that sweet nectar of truth that's ultimately who we are.

How Do We Communicate Our Needs?

As I write this, my daughter is ten days old. I'd forgotten in the three and a half years since my son was born that for the first eight months or more of life, babies say nothing, yet they're constantly communicating with us. Even at ten days old, when my daughter needs something she knows how to get it. When she's hungry, she starts letting me know by waking up. Then she moves around and begins to chew on her hand. If I haven't yet gotten the message, she starts fussing. And finally, if she hasn't gotten the nourishment she needs, she begins to wail.

We're all like this. It's our human nature. We have needs, and we have ways of expressing those needs. The problem is, we're not often taught how to evolve beyond our infantile methods of expression.

We also tend to expect others not only to understand our method of communicating our needs but to fulfill them as well. As adults, we have the power to fulfill many of our own needs for ourselves. However, when we do need support from outside, we can communicate that need clearly so that others have a chance to help us. If they can't help us, we have the privilege of looking elsewhere for support.

I had a friend growing up who was very needy. She needed constant reassurance about her decisions, her looks and her talents. She also needed constant favors, including the lending of money, which she never paid back. After about twenty years of friendship with what felt like very little reciprocation, I reached out to her after experiencing a traumatic event. I left a message on her voice mail telling her how upset I was and how I needed to talk. She never called me back. I don't know if she didn't get the message, if she got it and didn't think she could help me or if she just forgot. But whatever the reason, she didn't offer me the support I needed at the time. It wasn't until I realized that she wasn't going to call me that I finally recognized, as the country-western song goes, that I was looking for love in all the wrong places.

Maya Angelou said people will *show* you who they are. It took me a long time to see what my friend was showing me—that it wasn't personal. She wasn't ignoring me because I wasn't worthy—it was because she didn't have the capacity at that time to be supportive. I needed to look elsewhere for that support. When I really understood this, I stopped resenting her. I started to see all my relationships more clearly.

Now that I've learned to ask for nourishment from people and places who can give it to me, I think of her and remember the good times, the fun we had, the ways she did show her love and support. I also thank her for being one of the people who showed me that I'm much stronger than I thought and that, in many instances, I can take care of myself.

Many of us have to learn how to do this with the people whom the intelligence of the universe assigned to care for us. My mother always used to say, "God gave you to me to take care of. If he wanted you to take care of yourself, he would have plopped you down in a field somewhere." Sometimes the way our caregivers treat us makes it feel as if we've been plopped down in a field somewhere, but in truth, there's a wisdom at play that we don't always understand, setting us up for the next lesson, helping us learn to grow stronger so we can nourish ourselves.

Deep Listening

It's our job as adults to learn how to communicate, not just as a means to get what we want from another person but also as a way of connecting and offering support to others. A crucial part of communication is listening. Thích Nhat Hanh teaches the practice of deep listening, a nonjudgmental, non-interfering way of simply holding space for another person to release their burden. In an interview with Oprah Winfrey ("Oprah Talks to Thich Nahn Hahn", Oprah.com), he said, "Deep listening is the kind of listening that can help relieve the suffering of another person. You can call it compassionate listening. You listen with only one purpose: to help him or her to empty his heart." He went on to say that when we're able to listen in this way, we can see clearly that the person speaking has misperceptions about us, themselves and the situation. We can also see that we have misperceptions about them, ourselves and the situation.

My husband and I have only ever had one fight, but we've had that fight a hundred times. Each time, one of us does or says something to offend the sensitivities of the other. Then when the offended party points this out, the offender is hurt for being accused of offending. In this scenario, both of us end up feeling wrong and wronged. Over the years, we've gotten much better at recognizing this obstacle to our happiness and connection and choosing to let it go before a small battle turns into a war. Often, seeing that the other person just wants what we want—to be loved and understood—makes it easier to feel less victimized and more forgiving.

Every time I realize I've forgotten to do this, I renew my intention to remember, even in the midst of conflict, that we're both good and loving people who need a good and loving partner and to behave according to this truth. As my shaman friend Pete, who has been married for over thirty years, says, "Marriage is like putting two rocks in a tumbler and letting them tumble around and around until they turn one another into beautifully polished stones."

Learning to communicate can be like this. As Ram Dass learned in grappling with truth and love, we often have to tumble into one another, hurting and being hurt, in order to become the beautiful gems we were meant to be.

The Practice of Listening

Real listening is, in essence, a meditation. It's something that most of us have to practice. As children, we're taught to answer questions and possibly to ask them, but we aren't taught how to be present for one another in the answering of those questions. Most of the time, we're just waiting (though sometimes we don't even wait) for the other person to finish talking so that we can talk again. If we took out the words we were saying and replaced them with their meanings, much of our conversations would go like this: "Me me me me me me me me." "Me me me me me me me me me."

The practice of listening asks us to turn off the "me me's" and allow the expression of the other person to flow into our awareness. Unlike our personal meditation practice, opportunities to listen will occur without our planning, so we need to be ready at any moment. This isn't to say we have to spend hours listening to everyone who wants to babble on to us, but when we know someone really needs to be heard—our child, our spouse, a parent, a friend—we put down our distractions and our defenses. We open up to hear what's being offered.

We can start by taking a deep breath in and out. Saying in our minds, *I am here to listen*, or, *I am listening now*. Then we begin to hear the words the other person is saying. If they're physically present, we can notice how they hold their body, how they breathe when speaking. On the phone we can notice the tone of voice and the pace they use. Then we can more easily absorb the words they're saying. If this person is releasing a burden regarding another person, rather than agreeing with them or adding fuel to the fire by saying something like, "Yes, she did the same thing to me!" we can simply listen and offer empathy. If we instead say something like, "It sounds like that was really hard for you," we don't perpetuate misperceptions.

If the person is expressing grievances about us, it can be much more difficult to listen. As I said, this is something I'm still working on, but if we can take the "me me's" out of the equation, perhaps even imagining for a moment that they're talking about someone else, we can offer the same empathy we would want to receive in that instance. We can respond compassionately. "It sounds like that was really hard for you. I'm sorry you felt that way. I didn't realize I was causing you pain." When we're able to soften ourselves and offer understanding, the fire goes out. The person can't keep fighting us, because there's no fight to be won.

Recently as I was driving in Manhattan hunting for a parking spot, I saw one on the opposite side of the street. I waited for the light to turn red to avoid oncoming traffic and then made an illegal U-turn. I'm not saying that was a great strategy, but if I'd followed traffic rules, it would have taken me ten minutes to get back to that spot, which would most definitely have been gone by then. Just as I straightened out the car, I saw that a biker had run into the side of my car. While he wasn't obeying traffic laws either by running the red light, it was my fault because I pulled out in front of him. He started yelling before I even got out of the car. I took my time to park properly and take a deep breath before I got out of the car, and then I decided to just listen to him. While I smiled and breathed, he berated me, told me to go back to Jersey and said I was an idiot. Because I didn't know him personally, it was relatively easy to stay calm. I could see he wasn't mad at me. He didn't even know me. He was mad at the situation. When he was finished, I told him that he was right and that I was very sorry. I asked him if he was okay and if there was anything I could do. He looked at me as if we'd stepped into the boxing ring and I just put my gloves down. He touched his arm, checking to see if he was hurt. He wasn't. "Next time don't do that!" he shouted and rode away. Afterward, I was slightly embarrassed and a little keyed up but mostly surprised at how good it had felt to just listen and not try to talk my way out of it. This experience reminded me that most of the time when we're upset, we just want someone to hear us and understand.

Deep listening is also important when someone is expressing their hopes and dreams, sharing a special experience or recalling a victory. We often feel as if we aren't being heard when we have something to celebrate. As we saw in Chapter 5, sympathetic joy can be difficult to cultivate, so when someone tells us they've just received a new job offer and we're still working at a job we hate, it can be difficult to listen and be present. Remembering that the joy of another can be our own joy and that it can fuel the good fortune we want to experience makes it easier to practice deep listening. Also, again, taking the "me me's" out of it helps tremendously.

When practicing deep listening with a spouse or partner, we can actually set aside time to do this regularly as a way to avoid fights and cultivate clear, loving communication. In this case, it's useful to plan a time in advance and to make sure that when that time comes, there are no distractions. Then take turns speaking. You can even use an object, like a talking stick (or the remote control!) to make clear who's speaking and who's listening.

My English teacher in college brought a talking stick to class on the days when we read our assignments aloud to the group. When we held the stick, we also held the attention of our classmates. As we shared our stories, we felt heard and nourished. We can do this for our loved ones, too. When we practice deep listening with a loved one and they finish speaking, we can take a deep breath in and out. Then we can repeat back what they've said in our own words. Then we need to ask them, "Is that what you're saying?"

If they say yes, we can say, "I understand." If they say no, we can gently ask them to explain again. It may seem contrived at first, but when we practice, it begins to come naturally. We find ourselves becoming genuinely interested in what the people around us are thinking and feeling. We find ourselves feeling less defensive, with less need to prove our own worth and more open to another perspective and to truly witnessing the worth of those we love. I use a funny little mantra to remind me of this practice: "I'm stepping out of the 'me me's' and into the 'we we's.'"

Creating Connection

When my son was about three years old, we stepped out of the house to go to school, and he called out to a woman walking by, "What's your name?" She stopped. "My name is Irene. What is yours?" "Griffin!" he said, beaming. He has a natural knack for disarming people, getting them to stop what they're doing and connect. Granted, he's an adorable child, but I love how unselfconscious he is, how open he is to just getting to know someone for no particular reason. After I dropped him at school, I thought about why most adults (myself in particular) don't behave the way he does.

Often, we don't want to be intrusive. We may have a desire to ask, but then we think, "Why would this random stranger want to tell me their name?" We also think, "What's the point? I'm never going to see this person again." Or even more likely, "I might end up seeing them every day and being forced to make small talk when I'm running late for something!" All of these thoughts keep us from connecting to one another, connecting to the spontaneity that's available in the present moment. They keep us feeling separate and alone.

Even though it's not my first impulse, my son inspired me to start smiling and saying hello to each person I pass on the street in my neighborhood. I now do my best to make eye contact with the cashier at Target and the bagger at the grocery store and to ask them how they're doing. It makes a big difference to me. Sometimes I learn something new, and I always feel more connected. In a 2017 *New York Times* article, Jane E. Brody cites several studies showing that longevity and mental health are more positively affected by frequent social interactions and strong social ties than even by healthy lifestyle habits.

The medical assistant at my obstetrician's office saw me no fewer than twenty times over the course of my pregnancy. Each time she walked into the lobby with her head down and called out, "Flint, Elizabeth."

"It's Elizabeth Flint," I corrected. "How are you today?"

"Good," she would say, looking at her clipboard. "I just need to check your weight."

That was all I could get out of her. She'd become so accustomed to her routine that she wasn't seeing me as a person but rather as a name on a clipboard and a number on a scale. I didn't take it personally, but I did use it as a reminder of how *not* to interact with the people in my life, no matter who they are.

A few years ago, I attended a conference with a well-known life coach. In a crowd of thousands, somehow (maybe because I was jumping up and down, waving my hand in the air) I got picked to come up on stage to demonstrate an exercise for building connection. I was so excited you would have thought I was being called to "Come on down!" and try to win "a new *car*" on *The Price Is Right*.

I sat facing a beautiful young woman who spoke very little English. I spoke even less of her native Spanish. The coach instructed us to simply make the same movements and facial expressions as the other person. As we did our best to smile, touch our faces, clear our throats and breathe together, an incredible thing happened. The audience of thousands faded away. We ended up crying together and then laughing hysterically. We never even spoke, but by the end of the five-minute exercise, I felt as if I'd known her for a lifetime. I'll always remember Pilar and the time we spent connecting.

You can create connections easily using this method. It may seem strange at first to mimic someone's mannerisms or to try to breathe in sync with them, but it really works. They say we don't know what someone is going through until we walk a mile in their shoes—this is a way to walk in their shoes. By looking into someone's eyes and breathing with them, we can begin to *feel* with them, too.

Body/Mind Reconditioning Exercise: Creating Connection

The next time you want to create connection with someone, whether it's a prospective business client, a potential employer or your doctor, try these simple steps:

- Notice how the person is sitting or standing, and assume a similar posture.
- Observe their breathing. Are they breathing fast or slow, deep or shallow? Begin to breathe in rhythm with the person.
- Notice how they are speaking. Do they speak softly, loudly, quickly, slowly? Do they pause or ramble on? When you answer or ask a question, speak in a similar manner.
- As the interaction moves forward you can begin to lead the experience. You can actually guide the person to slow their breathing by starting where they are and slowly moving into a deeper breath. You can guide the pacing of the conversation in the same way.

Salespeople often use this technique to gain the trust of a prospective buyer. I don't recommend using the technique to manipulate anyone, because as karma goes, you too will end up feeling manipulated. I do recommend using it to feel more connected to people, whether it's a prospective customer, a co-worker with whom you may have a hard time communicating or a family member with whom you have trouble finding commonalities.

We often look at another person and focus on what makes them different from us, but we humans are about 99.9 percent identical to one another regardless of gender, race, age and status. When we focus on our commonalities, we create a connection that cuts through our false sense of separateness and gives us access to a power that's far beyond our individual selves.

As Maya Angelou writes in her poem "Human Family", "I note the obvious differences between each sort and type, but we are more alike, my friends, than we are unalike. We are more alike, my friends, than we are unalike."

Speaking Out

Studies show that the number one fear of most humans is death, followed closely by public speaking. Many of us feel that if we're forced to speak in front of a group, we might actually die. We're hardwired to gain acceptance from the pack so that we can be part of a group that offers protection and support. Speaking out, whether in a meeting at work or in a hall full of people, sets us apart from the pack. It sets us up for judgment and potential rejection. And the fear of rejection that most of us have is not unfounded. Most people, including myself, have had a less-than-amazing experience with public speaking at some point in our lives.

In eighth grade I decided to run for president of the ninth grade student body. There were no town hall meetings or debates, just one big speech in front of the whole school, after which the votes would be cast and the president chosen. I knew several candidates would be making their speeches with the Van Halen song "Right Now" playing in the background. I wanted to do something different, so I decided to impersonate Opera Man, a character Adam Sandler played on *Saturday Night Live*. I wrote out my speech on big strips of poster board to look like subtitles that I would toss aside as I finished each line. I practiced singing the speech in a false operatic tone to my parents the night before, and they laughed and cheered.

The next day I sat with the other candidates facing the audience, listening to everyone say things like, "*Right now*, I want to make a difference! *Right now*, I want to be your president!" I assumed that with my hilarious and unique speech, I was a shoo-in. But when I stepped onto the podium and turned to face four hundred of my peers, I froze. My face went red. My hands shook. I instantly came down with a near-fatal case of stage fright. I'll never forget the eyes of one of the popular girls from the seventh grade staring back at me. *If someone younger than me thinks I'm a loser, I must be a loser*, I thought.

The ominous music from *Phantom of the Opera* started playing. I did my best to pull it together, but I ended up singing my operatic speech to just one person, a friend who was sitting at the front with the line of people running for treasurer. (Unlike mine, she had a cute, safe slogan and speech.) When the music ended, I wanted to crawl under the podium, suck my thumb and wait until the gymnasium cleared out before showing my face again. But instead I sat down and closed my eyes, imagining myself at a new school where no one would know the horrors of what had just happened.

At the end of the school day, the principal announced the winners of each office over the loudspeaker. My name wasn't mentioned.

For the next fifteen years, any time I heard music from *Phantom of the Opera*, I started to quiver. Not until I started teaching yoga was I finally able to move beyond my fear of speaking in front of groups, and even now after teaching more than twelve thousand hours of yoga, officiating weddings and speaking in front of large groups regularly, I still feel a tiny wave of nervous energy right before I open my mouth. *What is that?* I wondered for so long. Now I know it as the deep-seated wanting of approval, an old friend that I can't fully relinquish but whom I can overcome every time I choose to do it anyway.

The Public-Speaking Emergency Kit

I've incorporated many techniques over the years to help me move through the fear of public speaking and into the authentic place within myself that longs to share with others. Here are a few of the techniques that have helped me:

- Imagine the voice of your biggest fan in your head rooting you on. Say to yourself the words this person would say to you. "You're the best!" "You're such an inspiration!" "People need to hear what you have to say!"
- Breathe deeply and feel your feet rooting into the earth. Imagine yourself like a huge tree, not performing for the audience but simply being with them in your natural beauty, strength and stability.

- When the voices of the haters come into your head, speak to them directly. "You are not welcome here." "Nobody asked your opinion." "Silence yourself! I'm speaking now!"
- Do the "Circle of Success" exercise right before you give your speech, make your presentation or lead your group.
- Tell yourself what my friend Scott from coaching school told me: "You are the Beyoncé of your own life." Because it's true.

Chanting Mantra

At the end of my group yoga classes, while everyone is lying in relaxation, I sing to them in Sanskrit. It always surprises me when someone comes up after class and tells me I have a beautiful voice. Growing up, I dreamed of becoming a singer like Whitney Houston or Belinda Carlisle, but every time I auditioned for a spot in a musical or a space in the choir, I was rejected. Not quite good enough, especially under the pressure and scrutiny of an audition.

Yet when I sing mantras with humility and devotion, I always receive the confirmation that I am in fact a singer. The swami who inducted me into the Sivananda Lineage in San Francisco called me a *bhakti yogini*, one who experiences the state of integration through devotional practice. Once while in India, I sat with a group of Shaivites (Hindus who worship Shiva) chanting, "*Om Namah Shivaya*," for twelve hours. Looking back, I really don't know how it was possible. I don't remember eating or drinking or getting up to go to the bathroom, although I must have. I just remember banging my little drum and chanting until the faces and clothes and scenery around me all blurred into an abstract mural of rainbow colors.

Sound is healing. Music therapists have great success with patients struggling with everything from eating disorders to Parkinson's. There's a reason why each chakra has a sound related to it. The vibration of these sounds sends a particular signal to the body to open up that energy center. This is why some Buddhist monks spend hours a day chanting

"*Om*" together. They aren't just changing the frequency of their own energetic bodies—they're changing the frequency of the world.

A man once came up to me at the end of class after I'd chanted the Gayatri Mantra, considered the universal mantra, and told me he'd been away from class for several months because he was sick with brain cancer. He said that in addition to traditional treatments, he'd listened to a recording of me singing Sanskrit mantras every night. He believed the music helped him heal. It was hard for me to imagine my voice having healing properties, but as I said, when I allow spirit to come through, it doesn't even feel like my voice. It feels like the voice of the divine singing through me. I believe we all have this power, regardless of whether we're pitch-perfect or tone-deaf.

Sound has great influence. When we hear a jackhammer while walking down the street, everything else comes to a halt. We press our fingers over our ears and hunker down. When my dog would hear the sound of a skateboard rolling down the street, she would lose her mind. My husband does voice recordings in a closet in our home, and for him every sound other than the sound of his voice is an intrusion while he's recording. I notice that even the type of music I listen to in my earphones greatly influences my mood and my perception of the world around me. This is why television shows, commercials and movies have soundtracks. Music gets you to feel what the director wants you to feel. Music evokes memories and hope for the future. Every religion uses music in some way. The music of voices is thought by some to be God's favorite form of praise.

This is one of the reasons mantra meditation is so powerful. The practice of mantra meditation can be approached in many ways. A gathering of yogis chanting mantras to music is known as a *kirtan*. These concerts have become popular in the Western yoga world through wonderful musicians such as Krishna Das, Wah! and Jai Uttal. Mantra can also be done as an individual practice where one chants aloud first and then repeats the mantra internally.

Eventually, the mantra you chant becomes something that's in your mind and on your lips all the time so that you're continuously aligning your mind and body with the meaning of the mantra. For example, if you chant the mantra "*Lokah Samastah Sukhino Bhavantu* (May all beings be happy and free)," which is pronounced "lo kah soma stah su key no bah van too," you not only send that wish out to others, but you also attract happiness and freedom back to yourself.

There are many different mantras in the yogic tradition. Some of them are Hindu, while others come from Buddhism. One of my favorites is "*Om Namoh Bhagavate Vasudevaya*," which is pronounced "om nah mo bah gah vah tay vah soo day viya." I learned from teacher and author Stephen Cope that this means "Thy will not my will be done." It's a mantra dedicated to surrender. By chanting this, we remind ourselves to let go of our habitual way of approaching things, especially when our habits are destructive, and to open ourselves to the greater wisdom of the universe.

The most powerful mantra for healing is "*Ra Ma Da Sa, Sa Say So Hum*." It comes from the Kundalini yoga tradition, which focuses on moving latent energy from the base of the spine up through the chakras. This mantra is referred to as the *Sushumna Mantra*. The *Sushumna*, the central energy channel of the body, runs directly through the center of each chakra up and down the length of the spine. This mantra is therefore believed to resonate in each energy center as it moves through the central energy channel. Studies have shown that when chanting this mantra, the glandular system and the nervous system respond favorably. When these systems of the body are balanced, healing can occur spontaneously. Users of this mantra purport that when they chant this mantra consistently for a period of twelve, twenty-four or thirty-five minutes, healing arises from the vibrations inside the body.

The Meaning of *Ra Ma Da Sa, Say So Hum*

This first part of the mantra moves up the *Sushumna Nadi* from the base of the spine to the crown of the head. A *nadi* is a channel through which energy moves, similar to a meridian in traditional Chinese medicine.

Ra means "sun." Sun is the ultimate life-giver in our planetary system. Without it, nothing other than fungus can grow.

Ma often means "water." Water is the other main nutrient needed by all life forms.

Da, meaning "earth," provides the soil, enriched by sun and water, where life can grow, heal and transform.

Sa represents air. All life forms need air. Even those that don't breathe air need the right balance of oxygen in the water through which they swim.

The second part moves from the divine realms, where it gathers healing energy, back into the body to disperse the healing effects.

Sa is the air, which sends the vibration back down.

Say is the totality of experience.

So is our individual identity.

Hum is the unmanifested.

I Am That

The mantra "*So Hum*," which means "I am that" or "I am one with the divine," is the abbreviated version of this chant, which is very useful in stabilizing the mind. One of my students is a kindergarten teacher who uses this mantra with her kids in the morning to help them prepare to concentrate.

You can practice mantra while doing your formal seated meditation or while you're walking down the street, going for a jog, driving, waiting for the train or sitting in the dentist's chair. Working with a mantra is often easier than following the breath. A mantra gives the mind words to focus on that not only stop it from thinking about other things but also direct the attention toward the essence or meaning of the mantra.

Formal Mantra Practice:

Sit comfortably in front of your altar or any quiet space that is free of clutter. Perhaps you have a singing bowl or some chimes you can ring a few times to listen to the vibration. When I ring my singing bowl at the beginning and end of every meditation session, I try to pay full attention to the sound, its resonance, its movement and the way it arrives, lingers and dissolves in accordance with the natural laws of the universe. This reminds me to treat the mantra that I chant with great respect.

Choose the mantra that feels most beneficial to you. I suggest working with the same mantra for several weeks to experience the full benefits before you incorporate something new. Some schools of practice encourage students to choose one mantra and stick with it for life. The benefit of staying with one mantra is that it becomes a clear object of meditation, showing us that it's not so much the object that influences our experience but our perception, which changes from day to day.

You can use *mala* beads (a string of 108 beads used for counting the number of times you repeat the mantra). You simply move the beads through your thumb and first finger one at a time each time you complete the mantra. The sacred number of 108 is generally used. I find that it takes twelve to fifteen minutes to repeat a mantra 108 times, so if you want to keep it simple, just set your alarm and skip the counting.

Start by saying the mantra aloud from twenty to twenty-five times. Then begin to whisper it, drawing the sound into yourself. Then chant the last fifty or so rounds silently. Keep reconnecting with the meaning. When you notice yourself going on autopilot, come back to the mantra with your full attention. Dissect the sounds in your mind. Put them back together again. Feel the meaning seeping deep into the cells of your body and the energetic threads of your being. When you finish, ring your bell or chime once more and notice how much more fully you can experience the sound. Then sit in silence for a few more minutes, observing the effects of the mantra on your body, mind and heart.

Informal Mantra Practice:

It's said that when Gandhi was shot, he used his last breaths to chant the Hindu name for God. "Ram, Ram, Ram," he whispered as the life force slowly slid out of his body. Ram is the embodiment of the perfect father. Gandhi had become so devoted to his god that he used his dying breaths not to curse the one who shot him or even to say, "Power to the people," in reflection of the cause for which he was dying. He used those last breaths to sing himself back to his original father, the one who created him, the one he could never actually be parted from and with whom he would experience a full reuniting in the spirit realm.

We all have mantras in our heads that we chant to ourselves all day long. "I'm going to be late!" or "I'm so tired!" One I used for a while was "What's wrong with me?" until I finally recognized that what was wrong with me was that I was asking myself that question many times a day. Every time I did, my brain came up with an answer.

Our informal mantras are probably the most powerful. They reflect how we feel about ourselves and our world. They also strengthen and solidify our projections. One of the most beneficial practices you can do as you go through your day is to use conscious, positive mantras. You may decide to take the mantra you use in your formal practice and simply chant that in your mind throughout the day, as Gandhi did. In this way, the mantra protects your mind from the negative thought loops and serves as a representation of all the positive thoughts you'd like to hold.

You can also choose to use an empowering statement as your mantra for a day, a week or a year. For example, as I mentioned before, whenever I start to feel the tiniest bit of illness coming into my system, instead of saying, "I hope I'm not getting sick," I say, "I am strong, healthy and vibrant." I say it over and over in my mind throughout the day. At first it feels untrue, and when someone asks me how I'm feeling, it's tempting to tell them that I think I might be coming down with something. But as the hours go by, I start to feel a shift. My mind begins directing my body and I begin to actually *feel* strong, healthy and vibrant, which makes it so much easier to say. I guarantee (because I've tried them all) that this works as well as any of the cold remedies out there.

Another way to practice informally is to use a mantra like "You are loved." You can say this aloud to yourself in the mirror as you get ready for the day. You can say it to other people in their cars as you drive or whisper it on the train on your way to work. People may think you are crazy, but who really cares? You can say it in your mind to the person speaking at a meeting you'd rather not be attending. When we say something like "You are loved" in a variety of situations, we break down our resistance to the people around us, to what's happening in the moment and, most important, to ourselves. If you repeat these mantras in your mind or aloud as you go through your day, you'll begin to notice big shifts in your inner and outer worlds.

Yoga Poses to Open the Throat and Connect to Our Truth

As the Yoga Sutras declare, our true nature is perfection. However, most of the time when we begin to examine our bodies, we feel that we're anything but perfect. When we look in the mirror, we see teeth that aren't white enough, gray hair, crow's feet or fine lines, bushy eyebrows and the like. Even the most flawless beauties we see on the cover of fashion magazines apparently have imperfect bodies that need to be airbrushed before their images go to print. This is what happens when we measure perfection by a standard that's not real. Nothing in the physical world can ever truly match the image of perfection we hold in our minds.

The good news about this truth is that it frees us up to stop trying so hard to attain that perfection. If we understood this truth, we might stop pumping chemicals into our skin to paralyze our facial muscles, sucking fat out of our thighs, dying our hair, bleaching our teeth and lasering our bikini lines in order to try to get to this imaginary place of perfection. True perfection, the kind the Sutras speak of, comes from within.

I once went to a Buddhist retreat center in Colorado and ended up sitting at a table of elderly nuns. I marveled at the fact that even with shaved heads, no makeup, hairy chins and unflattering robes, they exuded beauty. You cannot achieve that kind of beauty any other way than by learning how to fully recognize your deepest worth.

These yoga postures are offered as another tool. You can use them either to judge yourself—your appearance and abilities—or to experience the sensations of being in your body and the truth of your eternal perfection that's waiting in every moment to be recognized.

Dandasana with Jalandhara Bandha: Staff Pose with Throat Lock: Dandasana teaches us how to sit up straight on the floor. It asks the abdominals and back muscles to work together to allow the hamstrings to stretch as we straighten the legs. It's a great pose in which to practice Jalandhara Bandha (Throat Lock), which draws energy into the throat space, the seat of self-expression.

- ⊃ Come to sit on the edge of a folded yoga blanket.
- ⊃ Stretch your legs out in front of your body. Reach through the heels, bring your big toes together and point the toes to the ceiling.
- ⊃ Lengthen through the crown of your head and take hold of the back edge of the blanket. Straighten your arms and open your chest.

- Take a couple of gentle Ujjayi breaths (constricting the back of the throat as you inhale and exhale). Ujjayi breath is a mild throat lock.
- Inhale deeply with your chin parallel to the floor, and as you exhale draw your chin to your chest slowly, as if you're holding an orange under your chin and trying to squeeze out the juice.
- Don't round your back. Only the head moves.
- Hold the breath out for a few moments, and then inhale slowly as you lift your chin back to parallel.
- Repeat this five times. As you hold the breath out, envision *prana*, the vital life force that pervades the entire universe and animates your body and mind, circulating around the throat space, connecting you to your deepest truth.
- When you finish, come back to gentle Ujjayi breath for a few rounds.

Purvottanasana: Reverse Plank: This is the perfect counterpose for Dandasana, as it opens the front body, especially the throat space. I find it to be the most intense throat-opening pose because it requires upper body strength and attention to the alignment of your lower body in order to be done safely. You can modify this pose by bending your knees and doing a "reverse table" pose instead. If you have a neck injury, it's best to skip this pose. Instead, just sit and interlace your fingers behind your head, leaning your head back to open your throat.

- From Dandasana (Staff Pose), point your toes and spin your inner thighs down.
- Move your hands back about eighteen inches behind your hips and place them down flat, turning your fingers toward your hips.
- Press down into your hands as you lift your hips and chest toward the ceiling.
- While lifting your buttocks up, continue to spin your inner thighs down to keep your feet from splaying apart.
- Broaden across your chest and press down into your hands.
- Let your head gently lower back onto your trapezius (tops of shoulders) to open your throat space.
- Keep your lips together. This will prevent you from dropping your head back too far and compressing your neck.
- Stay here for three to five full breaths, experiencing the deep front-body opening.
- When you come down, slowly lower your hips to the floor and then let your head roll up, gently coming back to Dandasana (Staff Pose).

Setu Bandhasana: Bridge Pose: This backbend again creates the Throat Lock (Jalandhara Bandha) in a different relationship to gravity. When we practice compressing and expanding the throat chakra, we release stagnant energy, which allows us to more easily access our truth.

- ➲ From Dandasana (Staff Pose), bend your knees, placing your feet hip-distance apart. Reach your arms forward zombie-style.
- ➲ Tuck your chin and, using your abdominal muscles, slowly roll down onto your back.
- ➲ Once you're on your back, release your arms down by your sides, palms down.
- ➲ Keep your feet hip-distance apart and align your heels under your knees, pointing your toes straight ahead. If your lower back or quadriceps are tight, try placing a block between your thighs. Squeezing the block will help you activate your inner thighs and release pressure from the lower back.
- ➲ Press down into your feet and hands as you lift your hips up high.
- ➲ Hug your outer thighs in and spin your inner thighs to the floor as you lift your buttocks up.

➲ Roll your upper arms close together under your back. If you can clasp your hands, do so. If not, grab hold of the sides of your yoga mat and pull it outward as you lift your chest upward.

➲ Move your chest to your chin—not your chin to your chest, which could overstretch your neck. Make sure the back of your neck is not pressing into the floor.

➲ Stay here for five to ten breaths, strengthening your glutes and hamstrings. As you open your chest and the front of your pelvis, you're creating Jalandhara Bandha (Throat Lock).

➲ When you finish, release your hands and slowly lower your hips. Allow your knees to drop inward and place your hands on your belly to rest. You can then repeat this pose one or two more times or move on to the next.

Salamba Sarvangasana: Supported Shoulder Stand: Shoulder Stand is known as the queen of all asanas because it cultivates the queenly qualities of patience, strength and poise. It's also cooling, relative to other inversions such as Handstand and Headstand, and cooling energy is said to be feminine. Shoulder Stand is another pose that compresses the throat space. Because the body is inverted, blood flows easily down to the chest and throat, nourishing the vital organs, as well as the thyroid and parathyroid glands. These glands regulate our metabolism and our hormones. This pose also gives us a perspective of our own bodies that may not be the most flattering, so it's a chance to practice honoring your perceived imperfections as you uncover your true perfection.

I practice and teach this pose against the wall with two yoga blankets to protect the delicate tissues of the cervical spine (the neck). I highly recommend that you do the same in order to create a safe and effective pose. If you have neck issues or you find this pose too difficult, you can simply set up the blankets and the mat as instructed and then skip down to the end where you're instructed to rest with your hips on the blankets and your legs angled away from the wall.

- Make sure your two yoga blankets are folded into smooth rectangles the width of your yoga mat and about one-third the length. Yoga blankets, sometimes called Mexican blankets, are better to use than regular blankets. They create a firm yet soft foundation.

- Place the short edge of your mat at the wall. Then place the blankets with the folded smooth edge (not the white fringe edge) facing away from the wall, about a foot from the edge of the mat and facing into the room.

- Fold the end of the mat at the wall over the blankets, leaving about six inches of blanket showing. Then pull the whole shebang to the wall so that the folded edge of your mat is against the wall. There should be enough space on your folded mat between the wall and the blankets for you to sit on the edge of the mat with your left shoulder touching the wall.

- From here, swing your legs up the wall and check to make sure that your head is *off* the blankets. The edge of the blankets should align with the base of your skull where it meets the neck so they support the contour of your neck.

- Bend your knees slightly and place your feet on the wall.

- Press your feet into the wall and lift your hips as high as you can.

- Roll your arms together like you did in Bridge Pose, clasping your hands under your back.

- Bend your elbows and place your hands on your middle back, pointing your fingertips toward the ceiling as you press your elbows down into the mat.

- Hug your elbows into the midline and press your forearms into the mat.

- Draw your tailbone up and in. Stretch one foot up toward the ceiling in line with your hips. If that feels okay, try the other leg and then both together.

- Once both feet are off the wall, press your upper arms down and lift your chest up.

- Press your thighs toward the wall as you lift your buttocks toward the ceiling.

- Point your toes and align them above your hips so you can barely see them.

- Hold the pose for ten breaths. Eventually, you can work up to forty or fifty breaths to encourage a deeply therapeutic effect.

- When you finish, place one foot and then the other on the wall. Release your hands to the mat and slide your hips slowly to the floor.

- Scoot away from the wall so that your hips are on the blankets, your shoulders are off the blankets and your straightened legs are at an angle as your feet rest on the wall.

- Stay here for five to ten more breaths, resting and enjoying the experience of your royal feminine qualities of patience, poise and ease. When you're ready, bend your knees and roll over to your right side.

Salamba Matsyasana: Supported Fish Pose: This is one of my favorite poses. It's a gentle counterpose to Shoulder Stand, as it opens the chest and throat in a supine position. The supported version of this pose is a great therapeutic practice for those with kyphosis (hunched upper back) and anyone who spends a considerable amount of time looking down at the phone or the computer. It's also a great way to end this mini-practice because you can completely relax. You'll need a yoga block and your two blankets.

From the way your yoga blankets were folded for Shoulder Stand, fold each one in half into smaller rectangles and restack them. Place the blankets at the back of your mat to serve as a pillow for your head.

- ⮑ Place your block on the low, wide setting six to twelve inches in front of your blankets.
- ⮑ Sit about two feet in front of the blankets (with your back to the block and the blankets), with your knees bent and your feet on the floor.
- ⮑ Place your hands near the block behind you and slowly lie back, aligning the block under the bottom half of your rib cage. Your

head should rest on the blankets. Make sure you adjust your props if they're crooked so that you can relax fully.

- ⊃ Stretch your legs out long. Then lift your buttocks and lengthen them toward your heels before resting your hips on the floor again to release the lower back.
- ⊃ Let your arms stretch out to the sides, turning your palms up to open the chest.
- ⊃ Stay here for several minutes, resting and allowing the throat space to open. As you lie here, you can practice chanting the mantra *"Hum"* (the seed mantra of the throat chakra) a few times to create a vibration in the throat space.
- ⊃ When you finish, bend your knees and roll over to your right side. Rest here for a few moments before you come up to seated position. This is a great time to say an empowering statement about yourself, as your inhibitions are low.
- ⊃ Bring your hands to your heart and say, "I am powerful," or, "I am healthy"—whatever most resonates with you. Say it aloud three times with deep presence. Then chant the sound *"Om"* once before closing your practice.

Doing What We Say

"Happiness is when what you think, what you say and what you do are in harmony." — Gandhi

How often do we say we're going to do something and end up never doing it? How many times have you thought about taking that trip, calling that person, making that change to your diet and yet you haven't done it? When what we think, what we say and what we do aren't in harmony, we feel a discord that causes us to be in a state of *dis*ease. If we spend enough time in this place of *dis*ease, not only will we not be happy, but we may also end up being sick.

I had a friend for several years who always made declarations she didn't follow through on. *I'll call you tomorrow. I'll come to your class tonight. I'll stop by on Saturday.* The interesting thing was that these were all unsolicited declarations. I wasn't asking her to do any of these things. She was asking them of herself. She also had an eating disorder, and she would eat scant amounts of food in public and then go home and binge. I understood because I used to do the same thing, with both food and plans. I lost friends because of this, and I remember how unhappy I was most of the time. Her promises to call and be somewhere could just as well have been promises to eat only when she was hungry and stop when she was full. When she didn't follow through with what she said she would do, she wasn't just letting me down—she was letting herself down, too. Eventually, I stopped expecting her to do anything she said she'd do, and I stopped asking her to do things because I didn't believe that she would do them.

We've all been there in some capacity. We have the best intentions to go to a friend's party, but when the night rolls around, it's raining and we're tired and bloated and a party is the last place we want to be, so at the last minute we text or call to say how sorry we are that we can't make it. The bigger problem with this behavior is that how we do one thing is how we do everything. Eventually that escape clause applies to our exercise regimen and the training course we signed up for at work. When we don't do what we say we'll do, people stop trusting us and we stop trusting ourselves.

To be trustworthy, we have to learn how to be honest with ourselves. If the party is on a night when you would typically be too tired to go out, tell the host that you probably won't be able to make it and that you'd be happy to meet up at another more reasonable time. If your plate is already too full at work for you to take the training, tell your boss that while it's something you'd like to do, it would be better at this time to focus on the work you're already doing. This is a lesson I'm still learning. My dad says I like to "load my wagon," meaning I like to get involved in many things at once, often too many things, and at some point I can't keep up with them all.

Part of the practice of being honest with ourselves involves pausing and waiting to respond from a place of authenticity rather than reacting from a place of habit. When we learn how to do this, people will respect and trust us. We'll receive more invitations and opportunities than we ever would have otherwise, and we can decide from a place of clarity how we need to spend our time and with whom. This is a way of showing up not just for others but also ultimately for ourselves.

Honesty and integrity are the cornerstones of a life that's free of suffering. Resonance among our thoughts, words and actions creates resonance with our true nature. When we're in harmony with our true nature, we can effortlessly love everyone *and* tell the truth.

CHAPTER 7

Seeing Clearly Inside and Out

"All that we are is the result of what we have thought: it is founded on our thoughts and made up of our thoughts."

— The Buddha

One day when my husband and I were just dating, we sat in the depressing makeshift waiting room at the New York City Impound Lot waiting to pay $300 to get my car back. It was a rainy day and I had a cold, not to mention that I had two more yoga classes to teach after having already taught three. One would assume I wasn't having the best time. But as the man beside me made jokes, held my hand and profusely apologized for getting my car towed, I thought to myself, *If I can have a good time with this guy under these circumstances, we'd better get married.* A year later we did. In that moment at the impound lot, the fluttery feelings of new love trumped the annoyance of getting my car towed and the frustration of waiting for hours to get it back.

This memory reminds me that where we are and what we're doing is less important in creating our experience than our attitude is. Have you ever been in the middle of one of your favorite activities and still felt miserable? Have you ever been stuck in traffic or sick in bed and actually found that you were happy? If we don't consciously cultivate our moods, they arise unconsciously, and more often than not we *react* to our outer experience rather than *responding* from our inner wellspring of options.

It's not easy, but it is possible to tap into equanimity and positivity in any situation. When we do this, we can handle whatever life brings with much greater ease. My brother says that when adversity arises, he takes a moment to pause and look at the facts and ask himself, *Is there really anything happening right now that I cannot handle in this moment?* This is such a wise question to ask ourselves. We so often jump to what might happen in the future that we may not be equipped to handle, rather than stopping to acknowledge that right now we are, in fact, handling it.

Seeing things as they are in the moment is one of the most valuable abilities we can cultivate. It combats hysteria and overwhelm. It allows us to stay tapped into the natural state of well-being to which we're privy. In the shamanic tradition, the archetype of the great mother serpent, Sachamama, reminds us to see things as they are. As one of my teachers says, To Sachamama a stone is just a stone and a chair is just a chair. I take this a step further to say cancer is just a malignant cluster of cells, and bankruptcy is just a legal process. This cold-bloodedness may seem harsh, but another aspect of Sachamama is that she sees the true beauty in everything. Because she doesn't attach perceived meaning to anything, the true essence of what she encounters shines through.

However, if we live only at the level of the serpent, we miss out on the extraordinary experience of consciously creating our future selves. We must start on the ground, with Mother Serpent, seeing clearly, and then rise up to the level of co-creation, with Father Sky, where rather than just seeing what's in front of us, we envision our future as we would have it be.

This is the work of the sixth chakra, Ajna. The third eye, as it's called, is the energetic center related to our ability to both perceive the present moment clearly *and* create a compelling vision for the future.

In the Bible, Joseph exemplifies the ability to hold one's vision until it comes to pass. As a young boy, he had dreams of becoming a king. He shared these dreams with his brothers, who like most older siblings weren't especially interested in hearing about how great he was going to be someday. When Joseph's father gave him a beautiful coat of many colors, his brothers were so jealous that they sold him into slavery. (And you thought your sibling rivalry was bad.) Many years passed during which Joseph lived as a slave, but he never let go of the vision in his mind's eye that he would someday become a king.

Eventually, he did become a king and his brothers had to bow down to him. I'm not sure if they liked him more after that, but they could no longer deny that his vision had been clear and that he had a powerfully creative mind. Some call this the mind of God.

I like to think we're in a beautiful dance with the creator of the universe, constantly co-creating our future with the one who created us. When we surrender all our fears and limiting beliefs, we can glimpse a version of ourselves that's beyond what we're experiencing in the present moment.

In the shamanic tradition, we journey to the Upper World to witness the being that we're becoming, the fully realized version of ourselves that's waiting for us at the end of our journey. When I journey to the Upper World to see my future self, I often see a woman with a long blond braid sitting in a big white room of walls lined with golden books that stretch up into infinity. During my first few journeys to meet her, she sat with her back to me, looking out a huge arched window into the light. Now when I visit, she turns to smile at me. I can see clearly that she *is* me, perhaps in this lifetime, perhaps a hundred lifetimes from now. She is whole and complete and she knows it. She has written thousands of books in the service of the highest good and she has nothing to prove. She is simply sharing the love in her heart and the wisdom in her mind through the words in her books. This is the version of myself that I'm moving toward. After many journeys to the Upper World, now, like Joseph, who could always see himself as a king, when I close my eyes I can always see her and I know she is me, getting closer and closer every day.

How Do We Get from Here to There?

Many years ago, when I first read about our minds' power to shape our reality, I assumed that if I really focused, I could change things instantly. I remember sitting at a restaurant bar with a friend, holding the buzzer in my hand that would alert us that our table was ready. Having been told the wait would be over an hour, we decided to practice using our minds to get the buzzer to buzz faster. We stared at it intently and chanted "buzz now, buzz now, buzz now" for about ten minutes, but nothing happened. Fifty minutes later, it buzzed on its own when the table was ready. After this failed attempt at altering my reality instantly, I gave up trying at all for a while, assuming the Buddha had been wrong or my mind wasn't powerful enough to do it.

This is what so many of us do. We have a dream, we try a few ways of achieving it for a short time and then we give up, thinking it wasn't meant to be or we aren't good enough to achieve it.

The truth is that, like anything, shaping our reality takes practice. You didn't become proficient at walking, talking, reading or writing overnight. It took years of practice. You also didn't become an expert at expecting a certain experience overnight. Day after day of cultivating your habits has gotten you to where you are right now, so in order to change your life experience, you have to actively practice changing your thoughts on a daily, hourly basis.

To change our thoughts into beliefs that change our reality, we must first become consciously aware of the thoughts we're habitually thinking.

Thought Awareness Exercise:

Sit for a few moments in a quiet place and take a few deep breaths. Then ask yourself the following questions:

- When do negative thoughts arise? What time of day? In what situations?
- How do I feel when I think negative thoughts?

- When do positive thoughts arise? What time of day? In what situations?
- How do I feel when I think positive thoughts?

You may be surprised to discover that you start thinking negative thoughts the moment you wake up in the morning or when you're on your way to work. You may discover that you think positive thoughts when you're on your lunch break or on your way home from work. This may mean you need a new job, but it may also be an indication of your daily rhythms. Maybe you have more energy later in the day, which fuels your positive thoughts.

As a morning person, I wake up with a spring in my step, ready to take on the day. Around 3 p.m., however, I start to feel a little less confident in myself. By eight o'clock, if I don't actively cultivate positive thoughts, I might start to wonder, "What on earth am I doing with my life?" To work with my own rhythms, I've incorporated two practices. One is the practice of napping, which I highly recommend to anyone who gets the afternoon blues. It's like having a chance to be a morning person twice in one day! The other practice is working with a gratitude journal. You can keep the journal by your bedside and when you get sleepy at night, rather than turning on the news or a reality TV show, you can open your gratitude journal. Set a timer for ten minutes and just start writing about what you're grateful for in the moment. If you do this regularly, over time you'll become grateful for more and more people, things and experiences until you eventually find yourself being grateful for everything—even flat tires and stomachaches.

Once this happens, you're on your way to using your mind to create a compelling future. Why is this? Because it means you're able to stay in a state of gratitude rather than falling into a state of despair. In gratitude, you attract more good energy. In despair, you attract more depressing energy.

One of my clients recently sent me a text saying that when she dislocated her shoulder a few years back, she thought it was the worst thing that could possibly happen to her. But because of her hurt shoulder, she started coming to me for therapeutic yoga, which turned into energy healing sessions, which empowered her to make some dramatic changes in her life, including becoming sober after twenty years of alcohol abuse. She said that now she can look back and see that dislocating her shoulder was one of the best things that ever happened to her.

This is what the Yoga Sutras refer to as *pratipaksha bhavanam*— flipping the meaning of something we would ordinarily see as negative into something positive, which helps move us toward the highest vision we have for ourselves. My client's dislocated-shoulder example illustrates an important aspect of the creative process. We can't avoid challenges in getting from where we are to where we want to be, but we can experience more trust and gratitude in the process.

Visioning Our Future

"There are two kinds of people in the world: those who are dreamers and those who are being dreamed." — Alberto Villoldo, *Dance of the Four Winds: Secrets of the Inca Medicine Wheel*

As I walked through my neighborhood one warm summer morning, I noticed several people with yoga mats strapped to their backs and beautiful pink hibiscus flowers blooming in the yards of people who take pride in their homes. I saw several homes undergoing renovation and became aware that there was no garbage on the ground at the park. As I entered a sweet little French café with a natural-soaps vendor inside, I realized that I had envisioned this reality two years earlier when we moved into our new home.

When we first moved away from Brooklyn, where there's a coffee shop, a barber shop or a reclaimed-wood furniture maker on every corner, I felt a longing for that in our new neighborhood, where there seemed to be only Dunkin' Donuts, Subway and medical supply stores surrounding our new home. At first I complained about this and daydreamed about moving back to Brooklyn. My shaman friend actually said that when he tracked on my energy regarding our new community, he saw Edvard Munch's *The Scream*! I had no idea I was putting up so much resistance.

Shamans believe that we dream our world into being with the energy of our mind, so we can dream a nightmare or a glorious adventure into reality. After my friend told me about *The Scream*, I started to consciously imagine my neighborhood coming alive in the quaint way that made me feel happy. Every morning on my walk to the train, I imagined that the shuttered, run-down laundromat would become a rare-tea vendor and that the little window with the fading sign that read "Yolo's Deli" would become an artisanal coffee window for commuters on their way into the city. Almost two years went by before I began to notice that my dream was becoming a reality. The Dunkin' Donuts and Subway haven't disappeared (and, to be honest, I go to both sometimes), but as I explored the streets and parks with this dream in my heart, I eventually found the sweet little bakery, the sushi restaurant, the murals, the old churches and the rehabbed Victorian homes that create the urban vibe I love.

This is a small example of dreaming the world into being. We so often look around and see what's wrong with the world. We complain, we get angry, we even protest. What if, instead, we imagined, we advocated, we tapped into the feelings we would have when what we want has become a reality?

Instead of looking around your house thinking about everything that needs fixing, try closing your eyes and imagining it just the way you want it. Rather than looking at your bank statement and stressing about your dwindling funds, take the receipt that comes out of the ATM, cross out the number at the bottom and write in the number you want to see there. Then write "Thank you!" on the paper and put it in your wallet. As I said before, these practices won't change your life overnight, but if you're diligent, change will come.

One of my clients made a good living as a lawyer, but she was unhappy so she quit. In the few years after leaving her job, though, she didn't find anything to focus her time and energy on, which left her feeling lost and hopeless. When I journeyed to the Upper World for her, I could see a vibrant, peaceful woman walking with purpose on the beach. This woman moved with intention and grandeur. When I relayed the vision to my client, she had a hard time believing that this could ever be possible, so we started working on the conscious level with the Body/Mind Reconditioning exercise below as a way to open her mind to the possibilities available to her in the future.

She struggled with this work because she'd spent her whole life following the advice of her father, with whom she had a very complicated relationship. But as we all must eventually learn, when we live our lives the way someone else wants us to, we aren't happy. The gift of each life is that once we become independent adults, we get to live it as we choose. Beginning to see the possibility that she could actually do something that inspired her and made her happy set her on a new path full of incredible miracles.

Body/Mind Reconditioning Exercise: Creating Your Future

- Take out a notebook and write down the answers to the following questions: If you had no restrictions on yourself, where would you be in five years? What would you be doing? What would you look like? How would you feel? What would you do on a typical day? Where would you live? Who would be with you? What things would you have accomplished?
- Ask yourself, what are the limitations that are holding you back from doing this? For example: I can't travel the world because I have children or I can't quit my job and go back to school because I don't have enough money. Just go through all the reasons why you can't do what you would do if you could.
- Read over each "can't," crossing out any repeats that you may have said in a slightly different way. Then look at the ones that are left and notice the feeling underneath the obstacle. For example: If you can't take a promotion at work, is it because

you feel guilty working more hours? Or can you not take that trip around the world because you're scared to lose your job?

- Go back again and write down what your life would be like in five years if you let these obstacles govern your choices. Where would you be? What would you be doing? What would a typical day look like? How would you feel physically, emotionally? What accomplishments or experiences might you have missed out on?

- Go back to the limitations and turn them into possibilities. For example: If you said you can't travel because you have children, what if they came with you? What if you spent one week every three months traveling while their grandparents stayed with them? If you don't have enough money to quit your job and go back to school, what if you got a scholarship? What if your company paid for you to go back to school? Open yourself up to the "what ifs" even if they seem highly unlikely.

- Go back to the first question—If you had no restrictions on yourself, where would you be in five years?—rewrite your answer in the present tense, as if it's happening now. For example: "I'm waking up at the beach and going for a run. Then I head to my office overlooking the water for a meeting with my staff." Include how you feel, how you look and who's present, as if it's a movie scene from your life.

- Read your present-moment story aloud. It's even better if you can do this with a partner and have them give you feedback on any places in which the energy dropped out or you seemed resistant. You can also record yourself and give yourself feedback. Then read one final time with all the energy and enthusiasm that's needed to transform this dream into your reality.

I love doing this exercise every year in January. It helps renew my resolve to follow my dreams, to enhance those dreams and create new ones. Once I get to the place of feeling certain and enthusiastic about my vision, I record it on my phone and play it on my headphones every day for thirty days. This is potent medicine for the third eye.

If we're going to make it from where we are to where we want to be, we have to train intelligently and diligently, as we would prepare to climb Mount Everest. As part of our healing invocation in my shamanic training, we say, "May I step firmly onto the mountaintops I have only dared to dream of." To me this means: May I turn my dreams of the future into reality in the present.

Journeying to the Upper World

The practice of journeying to the Upper World is a meditation that takes us out of the time and space continuum that we hold as our reality, where we often have trouble seeing the possibilities for our lives, and into a place of timelessness in which we can see ourselves as the beings we long to be. In taking this journey, we capture an image of our highest selves and bring it back with us so that, like Joseph, we can hold that image in our minds even when we feel as if we're a million miles from our destiny.

A friend of mine has shared the amazing story of becoming the hairdresser for one of the most famous rock musicians in history. In her youth she worked at a salon where this musician's mother got her hair done. She frequently heard the woman talking about her son and how talented he was, but she figured it was just a mother's pride. However, when the woman suggested she call her son's girlfriend for a job, rather than blow it off she made the call, which led to the most incredible journey she could have imagined. Sometimes it takes only one stroke of luck, one synchronicity, to propel us to our destiny, but we have to be prepared to recognize and receive it.

I first learned the practice of journeying from the Four Winds School of Energy Medicine, but I've adapted it to suit the needs of those who aren't practicing shamans. (If you'd like to learn more about journeying and shamanism, please visit the Four Winds Society website.)

First you need to set up a fire for turning your excuses into a sacrifice for your highest self. You may want to reread the section on creating a personal fire ceremony from page 41.

We have to let go of our excuses in order to ignite our desires. When we burn something, the energy of the fire not only burns up what we don't want but also creates the pure energy to fuel what we do want. You can set up an outdoor fire or find a fairly large metal bowl to burn the paper indoors. If you're working indoors, make sure you have a cup of water nearby just in case the flames get too high. Some of our excuses hold a lot of energy!

- ⮑ Take a moment to sit calmly and take some deep breaths, clearing your mind and coming into the present moment.

- ⮑ Look back at the excuses you made to avoid following your dreams. Tear them out of the notebook one at a time. Read each one and say aloud, "No more." Then offer it to the fire. Watch it burn and disintegrate.

- ⮑ Take a moment to touch the space between your eyebrows with your first two fingers. Take five deep breaths as you connect to your inner vision.

- ⮑ Envelop yourself with white light, creating a protective shell around your being, so that as your energy body leaves your physical body, you'll be safe and protected.

- ⮑ Lie in a comfortable position on the floor or the ground. Feel the Earth under your body. Let your body relax into it. Take ten slow deep breaths into the third eye, holding the breath for a moment and then breathing out again very slowly, clearing your inner vision.

- ⮑ Now it's time for your energy body to rise out of your physical body. Imagine your energy body floating toward the sky (and up through the ceiling of the room you're in if you're working inside). Feel your energy body floating up through the atmosphere and into the clouds, the way you feel when you're in a plane that's taking off.

- ⮑ Keep going up through the clouds, through the atmosphere, as high as you can imagine, until you reach another plane. On this plane, your highest self dwells in harmony with all the highest selves of all other beings. To me, this is what heaven is.

It's not a place we get to by being religious. It's a state of being we evolve into as we remember the beauty and perfection of our essential nature.

↺ When you arrive in this place, notice all the beauty around you, the green grass and huge trees, the sparkling water and warm sun, the majestic mountains and verdant valleys. Like the Earth was before it was touched by human hands. Glide through this place, taking it all in.

↺ Then you'll come to a portal. It may be a gate or a door. It may look more like an opening in the sky. Rest here for a moment and wait for your guide to come meet you. When you meet this being, it will feel like reconnecting with a long-lost friend or a soul mate. Feel how wonderful it is to be connected to your guide, whose intention is to guide you to your highest self.

↺ Greet this being as feels natural. Look into their eyes and see the clarity and love radiating back to you. You can ask this being to guide you through the Upper World. Ask this being to help you meet your own highest self. If this being agrees, you can make your way through the portal. If not, relax and know that your highest self will be revealed to you when the time is right.

↺ If you are continuing through the portal to meet your highest self, notice a path that effortlessly pulls you to the place you need to go, like a stream of energy. This is how you know you're on the right track—no struggle, no resistance.

↺ Your guide will lead you to a dwelling—a house or a tree or a cave, or maybe an apartment or a castle. It's different for everyone. When you arrive, step through the doorway or opening of this dwelling. This is where your highest self dwells. Look around. Notice what you see. Notice what you hear and how you feel. This is the place where your spirit dwells always and forever. It never changes, because it is not a place as we think of a place on the physical plane—it is a dwelling in the realm beyond the physical.

↺ Look for your highest self. If you don't see this being, ask for it to be revealed to you. When you do see it, just notice how this encounter makes you feel. Whatever you feel is perfectly okay. Your highest self accepts you exactly as you are.

⊃ When you meet look deep into the eyes of your highest self. Feel the love your highest self has to offer to you. Feel the wisdom and clarity. Feel the peace that passes understanding flowing through your body. Just be in this space for a while.

⊃ When you're ready, ask your highest self some questions: *What do I need to learn? What do I need to do? What do I need to understand? What do I need to let go of in order to experience your presence in my life? What qualities do I need to embody?*

⊃ Just relax and receive the answers, knowing there is no judgment or urgency, only natural unfolding. As we don't think the flower is behind schedule because it's not yet in bloom, you aren't behind schedule if you aren't yet blooming into your highest self. This blooming happens naturally when we let go of resistance and allow it.

⊃ Ask your highest self any other questions you might have. You may get an answer or you may not. If you don't, trust there is a reason.

⊃ Thank your highest self. You can hug or bow to one another. Do whatever feels natural.

⊃ Before you part ways, ask your highest self to continue drawing you toward your destiny.

⊃ Then you can follow your guide back along the path to the portal. At the portal you can thank your guide for giving you this awesome gift. The gift of yourself!

⊃ You can slowly float back down through the atmosphere, through the clouds, through the air, down through the roof, through the ceiling and back into your physical body.

⊃ Take several deep breaths to draw your energy body back into your physical body, allowing your body to receive the pure energy of your highest self, to begin reorganizing to come into alignment with this highest self.

- ➲ When you're ready, begin to move your fingers and toes. Stretch through your arms and legs. Roll over to one side and come up to sit.
- ➲ Take a few moments basking in the glow of your highest self. Then write down as much as you can remember about your encounter. If you'd like to draw a picture, this can be very useful.
- ➲ From the words you've written, let the most powerful statement emerge. Turn this message into an affirmation that you can say again and again to align your mind and body with your highest self. Like the "*So Hum*" mantra from the last chapter. "*So Hum*"—"I am that." What are you? What gift has your highest self revealed to you?

In truth, there is no Upper World or Lower World in the energetic realm. These are constructs of the mind that help us to comprehend the vastness of what's present beyond the thin veil of our physical reality. To visit the Upper World is to take a trip to the place where opposites are no longer in opposition to one another but are rather two parts of one whole. The Upper World is a realm where you merge not only with your highest self but also with the divine.

Yoga to Balance Your Mind and Enhance Your Inner Vision

We illuminate the mind by working to create clarity within and without by striking a balance between our outer vision—seeing what's actually here in front of us—and our inner vision—through which we access what we can't see with our eyes.

The poses in this sequence will challenge your balance, which forces you to use your inner and outer vision to concentrate and come into the present moment. Through much practice, I've found that all balance poses are achieved through concentration. Once the body integrates the poses, they take less concentration, but when we're first learning, it takes everything we've got to stay balanced. This is analogous to changing our negative thought patterns into patterns that are more in alignment with our highest selves. At first we feel off balance when we change our thoughts. We can't grasp on to what we are used to. But eventually our new way of thinking, a way that opens us up to greater possibilities, becomes natural. In the same way as we practice balancing in various poses regularly, we begin to feel less like fish out of water and more like we're coming home into our true selves.

Urdhva Hastasana: Arms Overhead (Lifting and Lowering Heels):
This pose elongates the sides of the body, which in turn brings more space to the spine. Lifting and lowering the heels improves balance and strengthens the feet and ankles to prevent falls. With awareness centered on the *kumba*, the energy storehouse in the lower belly, balance becomes more attainable.

- Stand with the feet together so the legs feel united and stable.
- As you inhale, extend your arms out and overhead.
- Once your arms are overhead, keep breathing as you turn the palms to face inward. This will broaden the back and help you lift your chest.
- Soften the front ribs and abdominals in without shortening the waist.
- Find a gazing point a few inches higher than eye level. Feel the shape of the arms creating an extended energetic pathway from the Upper World directly into your body.
- Lift the heels on your next inhale. As you exhale, lower the heels and the arms at the same time.

- ➲ Repeat this five to ten times, synchronizing the movements of your arms, feet and breath.
- ➲ On the last round, keep your heels and arms lifted as you take five deep breaths. On the last exhale, lower your heels and arms, standing in Tadasana (Mountain Pose). Close your eyes and breathe, connecting to your inner balance point.

Vrksasana: Tree Pose: This most basic balance pose is one we can revisit again and again as our practice of yoga deepens. In this variation we explore different gazing points and closing the eyes to challenge balance and change perspective. If you have difficulty with balance or dizziness, please do this pose with one hand on the wall.

- ➲ From Tadasana (Mountain Pose), lift your right foot toward your chest. Turn your right thighbone out to the right.
- ➲ Place your right heel on your left inner thigh or calf muscle, avoiding the knee.

- Press the left hip and the right heel in toward the midline.
- Lengthen the right outer hip down, and lift the sides of the waist up.
- Press your hands together at your heart and find a gazing point straight ahead.
- Slowly raise your arms overhead. As you do, take your gaze up as well, connecting symbolically to a higher vision of yourself.
- After a few deep breaths, try closing your eyes. This makes balance more difficult. If you begin to fall, open your eyes.
- When you're ready, open your eyes and gaze forward again. Slowly bring your hands back down to your heart. Point your right knee in and release your foot to the floor.
- Take a few breaths before repeating this pose standing on the right foot.

Garudasana: Eagle Pose: This pose helps us embody the great eagle Apuchine, who can soar above all the distractions of our everyday lives and see the bigger picture. It is a standing balance pose that requires concentration and strength but also a sense of fluidity and ease. It's a wonderfully expressive pose because we first wrap up our limbs, binding tightly, and then we open them up like great wings expanding outward to take flight. If balance is challenging for you, you can try standing near the wall to work on the legs first, and then you can do the pose in the middle of the room, keeping both feet on the floor and working on the arms until you build up the balance to practice the arms and legs together.

- Standing in Tadasana (Mountain Pose), take a few breaths to connect to your inner balance. Then bend your knees and place your hands on your hips.
- Wrap your right leg over your left leg at the top of the thighs and try to wrap your right toes behind your left ankle. This isn't necessary, but it helps with balance.
- Open your arms like you're going to give someone you love a big hug. Then let that someone be you! Wrap your arms around your chest, trying to reach your fingers together behind your back.
- You may stay with this variation if your shoulders are especially broad or tense. Otherwise, release your fingers from behind your back and wrap the forearms in front of your face like vines twisting up to the fingertips.
- Lift your elbows high and sit deep into your hips. Find a gazing point just to one side of your hands and hold the pose for five more breaths.
- When you finish, unwrap your arms and legs as if you're going to fly away and then stand in Tadasana for a few breaths before you move on to the other side.
- Remember the eagle. The eagle symbolizes clarity, precision and expansiveness.

Ardha Chandrasana: Half-Moon Pose: As we walk to school in the morning on a clear day, my son often points out that the moon is still "awake." I look up to see the white outline of a half moon and remember that night and day aren't opposites so much as two complimentary parts of a whole. So I think of practicing Half-Moon Pose as an expression of unifying those complementary halves into one whole. This pose helps increase flexibility and strength in the legs while improving balance and creating a feeling of lightness in the body. You can practice this pose with your back against the wall if you need extra help with your balance.

- ➲ Begin with legs open wide (four to five feet apart). Turn your right toes out to the right and your left toes slightly inward.
- ➲ Place your left hand on your hip as you reach your right fingers out to the right.
- ➲ Look down and bend your right knee, reaching your right fingers down to the floor about eighteen inches past your right baby toe. If you can't reach the floor, place a yoga block on the floor a foot or so in front of your right foot and place your fingers on the block.
- ➲ Making sure your right toes are facing directly out to the right and that your knee is pointing in the same direction as your middle toe, begin to shift your weight to your front foot, lifting your back leg into the air.

- Press down into your right foot, slowly straightening your right leg.
- Straighten your left leg as well, reaching your left heel to the left, keeping it in line with your hips.
- When you feel balanced, start to stretch your left arm up, reaching your fingers to the ceiling.
- Draw your right hip back and in as you open your chest up.
- If you feel very balanced, you can start to look up at the ceiling. Otherwise, look down and breathe. If you have trouble balancing, you can come to a wall and do the pose with your back against it, sliding against the wall for support as you come in and out of the pose.
- When you're ready to come out of the pose, bring your left hand back to your hip. Look down and bend your right knee as you reach your left leg back and lower your left foot slowly to the ground.
- Stand up slowly. Straighten both legs and then turn your right toes in. Bring your hands to your hips and pause before repeating the pose on your left side.

Natarajasana: King Dancer Pose: Nataraj is the symbolic sacred dancer, eternally performing the dance between the physical and the spiritual, that which is formed and that which is formless. This is the dance we do as we journey to and from the Upper World. This pose is a challenging balance pose and a backbend. I suggest practicing with one hand on the wall until you feel comfortable letting go.

- Standing in Tadasana (Mountain Pose), place your right hand on your hip. Then bend your left knee, lifting your left heel toward your left buttock.
- Reach back with your left hand and take hold of the foot. If you need more support, place the right hand on the wall. Otherwise, extend your right arm overhead.
- Begin to press your left foot back into your hand, moving your heel away from your buttock as you stretch your chest forward.
- Keep reaching your right arm alongside your ear. As your chest moves forward, reach your right fingers out toward the wall in front of you.
- Draw your right (standing) hip back and your left hip forward to square the hips. This will stretch the left thigh more and take pressure off the right hip.
- In the full expression of the pose, your spine is in a backbend. Steady your eyes to one point in front of you and breathe deeply, experiencing the dance between the form and the formless.
- When you finish, slowly stand up and release your left foot to the floor. Stand in Tadasana for a few moments before practicing on the other side.

Breathing for Concentration: *Nadi Shodhana* (Alternate Nostril Breathing)

Nadi Shodhana means a breath that clears energy pathways. This breathing practice helps clear and balance the mind, which makes it a perfect preparation for meditation. Although it can be a little tricky at first to use the hand and fingers to direct the breath from one nostril to the other, over time it becomes natural. And as you practice *Nadi Shodhana* for several minutes at a time, you'll start to feel the profound effects on the nervous system and the mind. On a physical level, it helps to cleanse the nasal passages and promotes balance between the sympathetic and parasympathetic nervous systems. It also balances the two hemispheres of the brain. On an energetic level, it balances the yin and yang, or feminine and masculine, energies present in everyone. When these energies are in balance, the mind is much more stable. When the two main *nadis*—*Ida* (the lunar, or feminine, *nadi* on the left) and *Pingala* (the solar, or masculine, *nadi* on the right)—are in harmony, energy can rise safely and unobstructed up the *Sushumna* (the central energy channel, which correlates to the spine). So this breathing practice also paves the way for a deeper experience of our highest self.

If you have a deviated septum or nasal blockage, take care not to force the breath to pass through the blocked nostril. Just proceed gently, allowing some breath to pass through both nostrils to encourage the blocked side to begin opening.

Formal Practice:

Come to a comfortable seated position. If you have trouble sitting comfortably on the floor, definitely sit in a chair, as the use of the hand will make the practice even more challenging. Once you find a comfortable seat, sit up straight and take a few conscious breaths. If you find that your nose is stuffy, take a moment to blow it before you begin. Then bring your right hand up to your face, extending your first and second fingers. Place the first two fingers between the eyebrows, gently pressing into the physical location of the third eye. Place the thumb and third finger on the nostrils, but don't block them yet. Take a slow complete inhale through both nostrils and then gently close the right nostril with your thumb as you exhale through the left. Inhale completely through the left nostril. Then close the left nostril and open the right. Exhale fully through the right nostril. Inhale through the right nostril and exhale fully through the left.

Continue moving the breath back and forth from one nostril to the other. If you feel comfortable, you can begin to retain the breath at the completion of the inhale for a few seconds before you exhale through the opposite nostril. Once you find a comfortable rhythm, you may like to incorporate a mantra to help you maintain balance. I like to silently repeat, "*Om mani padme hum*," which translates as "the jewel is in the lotus flower," meaning the perfection we seek is already within us. I chant this mantra twice on the inhale, once during the retention and twice on the exhale. This helps me stay focused and keep a steady pace. The mantra is about four seconds long, so if you prefer, you can simply count slowly to four or whatever number feels natural for you.

Remember that the breathing should become subtler over time and less forceful. You can extend the breath and make it deeper without forcing it or making it harder. While you're breathing, you can imagine a soft stream of light the color of indigo pouring from one nostril to the other. Then you can begin to imagine it pouring from one side of the brain to the other. Finally, you can imagine the indigo-colored light filling up the Ida *nadi* and then emptying into the Pingala *nadi*, back and forth for the duration of your practice.

At first you may want to keep it simple and do the technique six to eight times using your right hand only. Then once you get more comfortable, you can increase your practice to ten cycles (inhaling left nostril, exhaling right nostril, inhaling right, exhaling left is one cycle) using the right hand and then ten cycles using the left hand so that one arm doesn't become too fatigued.

When you finish, slowly release your hand down and breathe equally through both nostrils for several breaths. Notice the ease with which the breath flows. Notice whether you can perceive a sense of greater balance and harmony in the body and mind. Sometimes I suggest practicing this technique before asana practice to help with balance. It's also useful before meditation practice of any kind to help clear the mind and develop concentration.

Informal Practice:

This breathing practice doesn't have an informal counterpart. It's a little awkward to do this on the train or while walking, and you definitely shouldn't do it while driving! Instead, just practice slow deep breathing in for four to eight counts and out for four to eight counts. You can incorporate the mantra "*Om Mani Padme Hum*" in your mind as you do in the formal practice while you're walking. I find this helps me stay present with the experience of walking or driving or even running. After several rounds of breath, you can practice pausing at the top of the inhale. If you're walking, it will be more difficult to pause, so perhaps save the breath retention for your seated practice. Once you have a steady rhythm of breath, you can start to mentally direct the breath from one nostril to the other without using your hands. This takes great concentration, but it is possible to psychically direct the flow of breath. Even attempting to do this develops our concentration.

Clear Seeing

"The only true voyage of discovery, the only fountain of Eternal Youth, would be not to visit strange lands but to possess other eyes, to behold the universe through the eyes of another, of a hundred others, to behold the hundred universes that each of them beholds, that each of them is." — Marcel Proust, *The Prisoner*

My mood becomes clearly evident the moment I step out into the light after coming up the subway stairs on the way to my office in the morning. Some days I notice the way the light glints off the windows of the buildings on Fourteenth Street, the way the city hasn't fully woken up yet and the air is still a little cool. Other days I notice the smell of garbage on the street, the grumpy faces of other commuters and the long line at Starbucks. It's the same scene, more or less, every morning. Only my mood changes. If I spend my time on the train sending loving-kindness to the other passengers and intending to have a happy productive day, rather than complaining about not getting a seat and worrying about all the work I have to do, I can see the beauty and perfection around me.

When we begin to notice our thoughts and change negative thoughts to positive ones, our perception shifts. When we journey to the Upper World and meet the version of ourselves that is already fully evolved and we're able to hold that vision of ourselves clearly in our minds, we have no choice but to come into alignment with it. We can choose to believe that who we are now, what we have accomplished so far, is all we will ever be and do. Or, like Joseph, we can envision ourselves as magnanimous kings and queens until our vision becomes our reality.

Our birthright is inner royalty. The path of yoga is often called "The Royal Road" because, if practiced thoroughly, it takes us from a place of feeling small, often disconnected and impoverished to a place of connectedness and true abundance. I encourage you to envision the possibilities for who you're becoming inside and out. The possibilities are limited only by the possibilities in your mind.

CHAPTER 8

Merging into Oneness

"I have come to drag you out of yourself, and take you in my heart. I have come to bring out the beauty you never knew you had and lift you like a prayer to the sky."

— Rumi, *The Soul of Rumi: A New Collection of Ecstatic Poems,* translated by Coleman Barks

I often find myself touching my daughter's head and lightly tracing the bony edge of her soft spot with one finger. The fontanel is the opening where two bones have not yet ossified. In French, the word *fontanelle* means "little spring." To me, this precious soft spot is the portal to the divine. I find it fascinating that just about the time babies begin to speak, the bones of their skulls finally come together to create a hard barrier between the inside and the outside, closing the portal. In the chakra system, the place where the fontanel sits is the energetic home of *Sahastra,* the crown chakra, our energetic entrance to the nonphysical world. I imagine that before we can speak, we remember what it was like in the unmanifest realm some call heaven. Then once we can use words in the manifest realm of the earth plane, our memory of being one with God fades.

One of my teachers told a story about listening in on his two sons' bedtime conversation. The older son, who was about three, said to his brother, who was just one, "Remind me what it's like in heaven, because I'm forgetting." This man said he stood outside their room and wept. We all forget what it's like to feel whole, to feel completely loved and fully connected. If we didn't forget, we wouldn't be here. No matter what occupation we choose for ourselves, our real work as humans is the work of remembering our divinity.

On a silent retreat I wrote a poem about this phenomenon:

Forgetting to Remember

I keep forgetting what I came here to learn.

I keep forgetting my divinity and yours.

I keep forgetting that it is not what happens, but how I see it that shapes my world.

I keep forgetting that true joy can only be held with an open hand.

I keep forgetting that this body is a transient shell, and I am just its caretaker for a little while.

I keep forgetting that getting my own way will not make me happy.

I keep forgetting that having more money will not make me safe.

I keep forgetting that true love asks nothing from another. It just is.

I keep forgetting that the only way out is through.

I keep forgetting that in knowing I've forgotten, I've remembered too.

Shamans believe one of the skills we must master is the ability to keep a secret from ourselves. When I first heard this, it confused me. Why would I want to keep a secret from myself? After sitting with the question in meditation for several days, I started to understand. Imagine stepping into a dark room, turning the lights on and being greeted with a booming "Surprise!" by all your friends and family. You thought everyone who loved you had forgotten that it was your birthday. So when you stepped into that room, the celebration was that much sweeter.

I for one am not good with surprises. I get an itch when my birthday comes, fearing that if I don't take care of the planning, it won't happen. I actually orchestrated my own surprise party in the sixth grade. Then on my twentieth birthday, I planned a dinner out with my parents and friends. Afterward, my friend Danielle suggested we go to a club, but we'd have to stop at our friend Rory's house to pick him up. When we pulled up, I thought it was a little weird that his house was dark. When I knocked on the door, I heard Rory yell, "Come on in!" I opened it and the lights flipped on to reveal a room full of smiling faces there to celebrate me on the anniversary of my birth. I was so moved I started to cry.

Being truly surprised is a real gift. To be reminded that we're loved, that we're worthy of celebration, lifts us up, gives us a clearer perspective and allows us to effortlessly embody the divine qualities we otherwise believe we must work so hard to cultivate.

This is why I imagine it's important to master the skill of keeping a secret from ourselves. We come into the world knowing that we are one with God as much as a mother is one with her newborn child. As we grow into physical maturity, we wane in our spiritual knowing. We must all go through what's sometimes referred to as "the dark night of the soul," a time of forgetting who we truly are and what we're here to do. Many people do such a good job of forgetting that they think they've entered the dark night because they have the wrong job or the wrong life partner. Or they assume it's because they live in the wrong city or they drive the wrong car. But when all these outer things are changed and the night remains dark, it's time to look up. It's time to start remembering.

How We Remember

"The true contemplative ... waits on the Word of God in silence, and, when he is answered it is not so much by a word that bursts into his silence. It is by his silence itself, suddenly, inexplicably revealing itself to him as a word of great power, full of the voice of God." — Thomas Merton, *Dialogues with Silence*

Two of the most powerful ways I've found to remember our divinity are through prayer and meditation. It's been said that prayer is when we talk and God listens and meditation is when God talks and we listen. To continue the party theme, prayer is like throwing your own birthday party and meditation is like having a surprise party. When we pray, we often do so because we want or need something. I distinctly remember my first self-directed prayer. Lying on my nap mat at a Christian preschool, looking up at the vaulted ceiling, I assumed God was just on the other side. I couldn't get to sleep, so I began to pray. "Please, dear God, bring either Michael Jackson and Hank Williams Jr. to my preschool." I imagined my two favorite musicians walking in through the door to the playground, Michael in his bedazzled blazer and Hank in his black cowboy hat and boots. What if they'd both shown up? Can you imagine if they did a duet of "Human Nature" and "Family Tradition"?

As I grew into a preteen, I prayed for certain boys to like me. As a teenager, I prayed that I wouldn't be arrested for certain misdeeds. As a young adult, I prayed that I would find my calling. As a mother, I prayed that both my children would survive spending the first week of their lives in the neonatal intensive care unit. Each time I prayed, God answered my prayers. It wasn't always the answer I wanted, but it was always the answer I needed in order to evolve.

I recently watched a documentary in which a Catholic mother learned how to ride a horse so she could join hundreds of Catholic cowboys, almost all men, for a pilgrimage to Cristo Rey, a sixty-five-foot statue of Christ at the top of a nine thousand-foot peak in central Mexico. She did this to pray for her son, who had sustained a brain injury in a car accident two years before. She said the fact that her son survived at all was a miracle. Now she needed God to heal him completely. She rode for days. Her husband and the son she was riding for followed in their pickup truck. When she finally entered the gates to Cristo Rey, tears filled her eyes. She kissed a small baby doll that's said to hold the Holy Spirit within it, and she prayed, "Please, God, heal my son."

Her son didn't miraculously stand up and begin talking to her again. It wasn't a biblical miracle. But when they went back home, she said she felt lighter. She said her son felt lighter, too. God may not have restored him to how he was before, but she believes he gave her family the strength to accept his current form.

Whether you believe in God or not scientific studies show that prayer has significant physiological benefits. It seems to be inherent in us to pray when faced with adversity. A University of Rochester study reported that when confronting a major illness, more than 85 percent of people pray. Dr. Andrew Newberg, director of research at the Marcus Institute of Integrative Health and a physician at Jefferson University Hospital, has conducted studies of Tibetan Buddhists in meditation and Franciscan nuns in prayer. He found that while praying, both groups experienced a decrease in the type of brain wave activity associated with a sense of self. They also had an increase in dopamine, the feel-good chemical in the brain. This suggests what spiritual teachers try to tell us: When we let go of the idea that we're a small separate being out here on our own and connect to something bigger, we feel protected. We feel a sense of well-being that positively affects our health.

A University of Cincinnati study showed that inner-city children with asthma who regularly practiced prayer and meditation had far fewer and less severe symptoms. Other studies have shown that those who pray more regularly overall have lower blood pressure. And a very interesting study done in 2009 by Ken Pargament of Bowling Green State University showed that when one group of people who suffered migraines were told to meditate for twenty minutes a day repeating a spiritual affirmation such as "God is good. God is peace. God is love," they had far fewer headaches and higher pain tolerance than another group of people who were instructed to chant, "Grass is green.

Sand is soft." These findings were reported in his thesis, *The Spiritual Dimensions of Healthcare: Bridging Research and Practice*. To me this suggests that prayer can't just be a rote or mechanical task. It must be something we approach with reverence and, as Hindus say, *bhava*—a spiritual feeling. It also points to the possibility that there is a divine entity listening to our prayers.

A potent prayer has three parts: validation, appreciation and supplication. If you aren't practiced in prayer, try to remember what it was like to ask your parents for something as a child or teenager. Demanding, groveling and bargaining usually didn't go over so well. What did work was first acknowledging the fact that they were your parents and you wanted and needed their permission or help. What really helped was appreciation. Only the very clever ones of us knew that if we wanted something from Mom or Dad, we were much more likely to get it if we first thanked them for all the wonderful things they'd already done for us. I'm not suggesting that God needs our accolades or that we should give them in order to get something in return. This appreciation is really to remind *us* of all the things the creator of the universe has already done for us, which not only fills us with gratitude but also helps us believe that God will continue to support us in the ways that we truly need.

As for the final piece—supplication—we may think it's obvious that a prayer involves asking for what we want, but in truth, many of us complain rather than ask for something specific. We tell God about what we don't want or we believe we aren't allowed to ask God for anything, because God already knows what's best for us. When we pray with validation and gratitude, we open ourselves up to receiving what we want. My sense is that God is always trying to give us what we want, but so much of the time we won't accept it.

For whatever reason, both of my children ended up in intensive care just after being born. As I sat beside the bubble where my son was being incubated, listening to the CPAP machine force air into his lungs, I slid a string of sandalwood mala beads through my fingers. With the passing of each bead, I prayed, "Dear God, please make my son okay." I repeated this prayer thousands of times. It kept my mind busy so that it didn't stray into the dangerous land of worst-case scenarios. And I believe that God heard my prayer. The creator of the universe received my unequivocal desire for my son to be okay. Five days later we took him home, and he's been exceptionally healthy, ever since.

Three and a half years later, we experienced a similar situation with our daughter. Although for different reasons, she was also sent to the NICU just two days after birth. As we sat in a different hospital room with a new baby, my husband and I couldn't believe we were in that same situation again. I felt scared, frustrated and powerless. The only way I could reclaim any sense of power was through prayer. Every hour on the hour, I took a trip to the restroom, where I got down on my knees on the linoleum tile and pressed my forehead into the floor. "I believe in you," I prayed. "I trust you. Thank you for healing my daughter. Thank you for bringing her home as quickly as possible. Thank you for giving her a long, healthy, happy life." Seven days later, we brought her home and she's been beyond perfect ever since.

Though I don't know why both my children ended up in the NICU, I do know without a shadow of a doubt that my prayers were answered. And I don't think it was because I deserve healthy kids more than someone whose kids are not healthy or have passed away. Ultimately, God is a mystery. But I do think that my clearest desire for them to be healthy aligned with their own clearest desires to be healthy and that because we were both in alignment, this helped them survive and thrive.

Almost thirty years ago when my brother was sixteen, he crashed his pickup truck into a tree, killing his passenger on contact. The doctors said my brother would certainly die within twenty-four hours. When those twenty-four hours passed, they said forty-eight and so on. My mother sat at his bedside for four months while he was in a coma surviving on a ventilator. She prayed fervently, "Dear God, make my baby okay. Help him walk out of here. Heal his body."

Her prayers were answered. Against all odds, he survived. He sustained permanent injuries to the brain, but he learned how to walk and talk again. Like the boy whose mother rode to Cristo Rey, his brain never fully healed from the damage, but for many years he lived on his own. Only recently was he moved into an assisted living home where he can receive the care he now needs.

The movements and motives of the divine are so far beyond our comprehension that it does no use to ask "Why?" I find it so much more useful to look at the way in which my prayers have been answered and to pour myself into gratitude for those answers, even when they aren't the ones I wanted.

Sometimes we want something so much, like to marry someone we love, and it doesn't happen. Perhaps this is because it wouldn't be the best thing for the person we love or, on some level, we know it wouldn't be the best thing for *us*. When my best friend fell ill after a lung transplant, as much as I wanted to pray for him to make it, I could feel that he was ready to go. He actually came to me in a dream the night he died and said, "It's all right, dude." He was ready to let go of the body that was no longer working. If we had kept praying for him to survive, we would have been praying against his wishes.

This brings me to a prayer that I only recently began to embrace. One of my shaman mentors prays, "Show me; teach me." Praying this prayer is easy when things are going well, when we're open and ready to learn from life. It's not easy when life is moving in one direction and we want so badly for it to move in another. This prayer requires us to let go. It asks us to stop planning our own surprise party and to open up to the possibility that the creator of the universe knows a thing or two about throwing parties. I'm not suggesting that the death of a loved one is a party by any means, but perhaps if we trusted God enough to believe that we'll never be forsaken, we could see that death is simply a letting go of the forgetfulness of the body and a full reuniting with the remembrance of our divinity.

How to Pray

There are many ways to pray. Some suggest that the Lord's Prayer is the only prayer we ever need to pray. Others suggest prayer is a conversation with God that's different every time. And as Meister Eckhart said, "If the only prayer you ever say in your entire life is, 'Thank you,' this would be enough."

My own experience points to the model I suggested above: acknowledge, appreciate and supplicate. For example, "Dear God (just using this opening acknowledges the creator's potency), thank you for every single moment of every single day of my life. Thank you for all the lessons, all the joys and all the experiences that have brought me to this moment—now. (Appreciation helps us to remember our past prayers' being answered and to open up to the answering of our current prayers.) Please show me how and help me to be the most loving version of myself in all situations. (Supplication is the last step.)"

This may seem simple, but I promise you it's very powerful. When you pray this kind of prayer, God will show up as your neighbor spouting sexist remarks to you on your way to work. God will show up as your boss demoting you in order to give her niece your position. God will show up as the guy who cuts you off in traffic when you're already late for your appointment. God will show you all the places in which you're not being the most loving version of yourself so that you can clean up your act. This is why many people think prayer doesn't work.

You may be thinking, "But I prayed to be loving and I feel like a total jerk! It's not working." Trust me. This is the way many prayers are answered. Only from going through this process myself again and again, do I know that we must see the places where we're being, doing or having what we *don't* want in order to be, do and have what we *do* want. It's like saying you want a clean house. What do you do to get a clean house? You look for all the dirt, and when you find it, you get rid of it. Then the house is clean.

Listening to God

When we start to pray these kinds of prayers, we're getting closer to the other side of our conversations with God, which is the listening. Can you imagine being out to lunch with the creator of the universe and all you do is sit there blabbing on about your problems and how you need help with fixing them? Wouldn't it be wiser to shut your mouth and hear what the highest intelligence of the universe has to say? You'd think so, but it's very difficult for us forgetful humans to be quiet and listen.

The second Yoga Sutra says, "Yoga is the cessation of the whirling of the mind." Our minds are constantly whirling, which makes it very difficult to stop and listen to anything, especially a voice that we can't hear with our ears but only with our hearts. However, the third Sutra says that when we do achieve the state of yoga, or the cessation of the whirling mind, our true and perfect nature is revealed. To me, this means that the God within us is revealed. The secret we've been keeping from ourselves, the biggest secret of all, that we are one with God, is revealed through the most exquisite surprise party ever.

But like all great parties, this one takes a lot of planning. We don't just sit down one day and say, "Okay, mind, stop whirling so I can hear God." That would be like saying, "Okay, legs, let's run this marathon!" without any training.

Training for a marathon means running a few miles a day for a month, then a few more miles a day for another month and so on until our legs and heart and breath sync up to allow us to run 26.2 miles without stopping.

Training to listen to God means sitting quietly for five minutes a day, then ten, then fifteen, then twenty and so on until our minds are still enough to hear that soft voice emanating from the center of our hearts. It's not so much about the amount of time we spend sitting but about the amount of attention we give to the time we spend sitting. If you just set your alarm and sit still but all you do is plan your grocery list, you won't hear the voice of God. If you sit still and fall asleep, you'll miss the beautiful wisdom that's waiting for you. But if you sit still and follow your breath moving in and out, if you drop the thoughts that arise, let go of the judgments that come up, release the plans you're making, the mind, like a puppy, will eventually get tired of trying to run away. It will sit still and it will listen.

And when it does, it's sweeter than any romance you've ever experienced. It's like looking into the eyes of a new baby and not just seeing the baby you love but seeing yourself as lovable as that baby and seeing the creator that created you both, smiling in satisfaction at its creation. There's a story in the Bhagavad Gita that says when Krishna was a baby, his mother looked into his mouth and witnessed the entire cosmos. She was so overwhelmed that she couldn't function. And because he, an embodiment of the divine, loved her so much, he veiled her eyes with a mother's love so she no longer saw her child as an avatar but just as the beautiful baby she knew and loved. Only when we're ready will we hear God's voice and see God's face.

Why We Don't Listen

If listening to God is so blissful, why don't we do it more often? There are many reasons for this. For starters, we've been taught not to trust the voice of God. We've been taught to trust outside voices telling us what to do, where to go and how to feel, based on the cultural consciousness of the time. We've been told that God doesn't speak to us directly—God speaks to us only through books written by people who lived a long, long time ago or maybe through godly people like priests and saints.

We may also confuse the critic in our head with the voice of God. This confusion is understandable. Wouldn't it make sense that the God we've been taught to fear, the one who needs us to do something specific to be loved, the one who punishes us when we do something wrong, would be a tad bit critical?

The way I distinguish the voice of God from the critic is simple. The critic makes me feel small, separate, unworthy and foolish, not to mention strapped for cash, time and expertise. The voice of God makes me feel supported, connected, expansive, powerful and unabashedly loved beyond anything I've ever experienced.

The voice of God does offer guidance, and sometimes it suggests we do things that we may not feel like doing, say things we may not feel like saying, let go of things we may not feel like letting go of. But these suggestions are only designed to bring us into deeper alignment with our true nature, not to cut us off from our divinity the way the critic does.

When you sit and listen, you'll know whether you're listening to God or the inner critic by how the inner voice makes you feel. If you feel loved, it's God. If you feel in any way unloved, it's the critic. My grandmother calls this voice the Devil. And while that word doesn't work for me, I understand why she uses it. That critic *is* a little devil that tries to get between God and us. But rather than fearing it or going to battle with it, we can simply stop giving our energy to it and start giving our energy to the divine. I believe that when the Bible suggests that God commands us to love "him" above all others, this isn't because God is needy and jealous. It's because God knows that divine love is the source of all love. God also knows that to receive love, we must give love. So why not give love to the source of all love so that we can then experience it in its purest, most potent form?

Also, when we love God with all our minds and all our hearts and all our souls, it's pretty hard to break any of the other commandments. When we're in love with God, we don't feel the need to kill somebody or play secret wife swap with the neighbors. Listening to God and loving God are one and the same. When we listen, we love. When we love, we listen.

How We Listen

It's not as easy to listen to the voice of God as we might like. It's a soft and subtle whisper among the cacophony of the mind and the external world. This is why people go into monasteries and practice silence. There's a cloister of nuns in Missouri who adhere to silence for seventeen of their eighteen waking hours a day. They don't spend that one hour chatting about the goings on at the convent or what Sister Mary did to Sister Ruth last night at dinner. They spend that one hour singing praise to their heavenly love, whom they recognize as Jesus Christ. When you hear their angelic voices, the purity of devotion can make you cry.

Most of us won't be joining a silent order any time soon. Especially if you have one of those things called a job or you live with one of those humans called a child. (Children are silent only when they're sleeping and, sometimes, chewing.) We can, however, practice moments of silence throughout the day. As tough as it sometimes is to unplug, there are always opportunities in the day to do so. When we have fifteen minutes before our next conference call. When we're waiting in line to pick up our kids from school. When we're stuck in traffic on the way home from work. Instead of turning on the radio or calling a friend, we turn the dial to the God channel.

It may sound strange, but after practicing this many times, I honestly feel that the moment I quiet down my mind and say, "Hi, God," God says, "Hi," right back. I know that it's God because it feels as if my best friend in the world has just picked up the phone. Once I hear that "Hi" on the inside, I just ask a question. Here are a few examples you might try:

- How can I be of service today?
- What am I not understanding about this situation?
- How can I best support my kids, spouse, boss in this situation?
- What do I need to do right now to let this go?
- How can I bring more joy, abundance and community into my life?

The trick is, once you've asked the question, you have to be willing to listen to the answer. It may not be what you hoped for, though. In most cases it's not, because if it were, you probably would have already done it or understood it. For example, if you ask how you can best support your spouse in a certain situation and the answer you receive is, "You can stop being judgmental and give him or her your unconditional support," you might be just a little resistant, especially if you believe you really know what they should be doing that they aren't doing. The truth is, only God knows what any other person should or shouldn't be doing. Our opinions about other people come from a very limited perspective.

A great way to know if the voice you heard was the voice of God is to do what it said and see what happens. Maybe, just maybe, if you give your spouse unconditional support, he or she will feel that. It will make them stronger and they'll end up doing what you thought they should have done in the first place. God may actually offer you a different approach to get the results you truly want.

Know this: God is speaking to all of us all the time. The less we listen, the more trouble we have in life, not because we're being punished but because we aren't in alignment with the power source of the universe. The more we listen, the more joy, peace and abundance we experience, regardless of our outer circumstances, because we're plugged in to the divine source.

If you have trouble quieting your mind enough to listen, I suggest starting with a ten-minute breath-centered meditation to clear your mind of distractions. You can download one of the meditations from my website: **www.e-yoga.com/audio**. You can also follow the simple instructions below.

Formal Practice:

Find a comfortable seated position, either on the floor or in a chair. Sit up tall, resting your hands on your lap. Close your eyes. Lengthen your spine, pressing down into your sitting bones and lifting up through the crown of your head. Broaden across your collarbones and soften your shoulder blades down your back. Relax the space between your eyebrows and soften your jaw. Begin to notice the breath moving in and out of your nostrils. Notice the sensation of breath coming in and the sensation of breath going out.

Thoughts will come into your mind. Don't fight them. Just let them drift into the background as you give your attention to your breath. Follow the inhale moving in and the exhale moving out. Don't try to control the breath. Just let it flow in and out. Imagine your mind like a riverbed allowing the river of your breath to flow through it. No need to stop it or control it. Just watch the breath flow in and out of your nostrils. *Pause.*

Feel the breath move in and out of your chest. *Pause.*

Notice the belly expand and contract as you breathe in and out. *Pause.*

Relax your whole body, feeling the energy of the breath flow through you without any resistance at all. *Pause.*

Continue to follow the flow of the breath for a few more minutes until your mind settles down. When you're truly ready to listen, call on the divine. God doesn't use voice mail; God always answers. The first thing you hear, the thing that seems too simple to come from the voice of God, is most likely the most profound and poignant guidance you'll receive. Rather than ignore what seems simple, cliché or unclear, ask more questions:

- What does this have to do with me?
- How do I do this?
- How will I know when or where to do this?

Answers will follow. Trust them the way you'd trust a map. The guidance of God is the most accurate GPS you could find. I'm probably not the only one to think of this, but I like to call it the God Positioning System. If the creator of the universe can see everything that ever was and will be, don't you think it's pretty good at directing you where to go and giving you the best route to get there?

As one of my mentors says, trust and follow. Don't let your mind get in the way of God's voice. Let God's voice take up residence in your mind.

Resting in Infinity

There's a space even beyond conversing with God. In yoga philosophy it's known as Samadhi. In the Buddhist religion it's called Nirvana. In Christianity it's referred to as Christ consciousness. It's the space in which the body fades from our awareness and time is irrelevant. The mind slows down so much that it becomes quiet. The word for *stop* in Sanskrit is *nirodaha*. When the mind stops, Samadhi arises. When the mind stops, God rushes in.

I believe that when Jesus said, "I am the way, the truth and the light," he was saying that he had so fully merged with the divine that he and his heavenly father had become one and the same. Many people would disagree with me, but I believe that each one of us can merge with the divine.

As I mentioned earlier, while in India I chanted, "*Om Namah Shivaya, Om Namah Shivaya,*" for hours and hours every day. During a few of these sessions I completely lost track of time. Once I sat chanting for four hours and could have sworn it had been thirty minutes. As I said in Chapter 6, I chanted with a group of Shaivites for twelve hours straight, stopping only to drink water and pee. If someone had told me we would be there for twelve hours, I never would have made it. But something about repeating the same phrase over and over eventually cleared my mind of its obsession with time and its fixation on "me and mine." I drifted out of my body and into oneness with spirit.

It's hard to explain the experience of merging. It's beyond what the mind can comprehend and what words can explain. Ramana Maharshi said that when he tried to explain the experience of Samadhi to his students, something shut his mouth. Not only does trying to explain it dissipate the energy of the experience, but it can also cause others to go looking for a replication of someone else's experience. If your trusted teacher tells you it happens in a certain way, you might deny your experience if it happens in another way. Moreover, you may feel that if you don't have the experience at all, you aren't worthy.

I believe that the experience of merging with the divine or resting in infinity is as different as the individual, but with one unifying characteristic: Time and space disappear and a pervading sense of peace takes over. It's said that we can't find enlightenment by looking for it, but if we don't look for it we won't find it. This points to the yogic philosophy of effort and surrender: Abhyasa and Vairyaga. If we just sit around eating ice cream and watching television, we definitely won't merge with the divine. We must practice daily, opening our bodies and our hearts and quieting our minds. But we also can't force grace to come to us. When the fruit is ripe, as they say, it will fall from the tree. Our practice ripens us, prepares us for the experience of merging. But in the end, only when we let go completely, even of the practice, can we truly merge.

Yoga Poses to Cultivate Oneness

Sahasrara, the crown chakra, is located at the top of the head. It's the energy center that spirit enters to breathe its life into us. When the crown chakra is open, free of blockages, not mired by dense energy, we can effortlessly commune with God. The following poses will help you physically prepare the crown chakra for the experience of resting in the God space. If you have a neck injury, high blood pressure or glaucoma, skip the headstand and work with a qualified teacher on alternative poses.

Virasana with Gomukhasana Arms: Hero's Pose with "Cow Face" Arms: This pose aligns the spine and helps prepare the shoulders for Headstand. Also, when we bind the hands together we can experience the oneness that binds the individual self to the universal self. You may need a strap for your hands.

- ⮎ Start from a kneeling position with your knees together. Place a yoga block or folded blanket between your ankles and sit on that elevated surface.
- ⮎ Lengthen down through your tailbone and up through the crown of your head. Broaden your collarbones. Connect to the subtle energy running up and down the length of your spine. Imagine the energy moving up your spine as you inhale and down your spine as you exhale.
- ⮎ Place the strap over one shoulder. Reach your right arm up by your ear, turning your palm to the back of the room. Bend your elbow and reach down between your shoulder blades for the strap.
- ⮎ Stretch your left arm out to the side. Turn your palm to the back and bend your elbow down by your side, sliding your hand up your back to find the strap.
- ⮎ Once you're holding the strap (or clasping your fingers, if you can reach easily), re-lengthen your spine. Soften your front ribs in and lift your back ribs up.
- ⮎ Close your eyes and imagine your arms like an energy circuit running from your heart up through your right arm, down to your left fingers, through your left arm and back to your heart like a Möbius strip.
- ⮎ Stay here for ten breaths. Then release your arms, pausing for a few moments before you switch arms and repeat the visualization of energy moving through your arms the way it moves through infinity.
- ⮎ When you finish both sides, sit for another few breaths with your hands in your lap before moving on to the next pose.

Adho Mukha Svanasana: Downward-Facing Dog Pose: This pose has been suggested in several chapters for various reasons. In working with our connection to the universe, Downward Dog sends energy toward the crown of the head, where the crown chakra resides. While it prepares the arms, shoulders and hamstrings for Headstand, it is also a good alternative to Headstand if you have a neck injury or difficulty getting into Headstand.

See previous chapters for instructions.

- When in the pose, close your eyes and focus on the movement of energy from the tailbone to the crown of the head. Imagine your crown chakra being cleared to allow the light of the divine to shine in.
- Stay in the pose for ten to twenty breaths. Then rest in Balasana (Child's Pose) before attempting Sirsasana (Headstand).

Sirsasana: Headstand: This pose is traditionally called the king of all asanas. As a worthy king wears his crown with both confidence and humility, we all have a birthright of royalty available to us. When we become comfortable in Sirsasana, we can experience our inner royalty, and as BKS Iyengar taught, when we hold the pose comfortably for an extended period of time our "inner luster" shines forth. I had a friend in yoga school who held this pose for an hour every day, and he certainly had an inner luster that shone out on everyone he met.

If you aren't able to practice Headstand, you can do Adho Mukha Svanasana (Downward-Facing Dog) as mentioned above or a wide-legged standing-forward bend with a block under the crown of the head to feel the connection to the earth through the crown chakra.

Sirsasana (Headstand) is a pose of reverence, bowing to that inner divinity that we didn't create but rather was instilled in us by our creator. When we approach the pose with reverence, we're much less likely to cause injury. This means listening to your body and coming out of the pose when you need to, slowly and safely. I recommend learning the pose initially from a qualified teacher. It's best to do this pose near the wall when you first learn in order to maintain balance, but over time you can practice the pose without the support of the wall.

- From Balasana (Child's Pose), lift your head. Wrap your hands around your elbows to measure the distance, making sure the elbows are shoulder distance apart.
- Interlace your fingers and press your forearms and wrists into the floor.
- Place the very center of the crown of your head on the floor, with the back of your head touching your hands.
- Lift your hips and knees as you press your forearms down. Lift your shoulder blades up your back to create stability and space in your neck.
- Walk your feet toward your elbows as you continue to press your shoulder blades into your back.
- Draw one knee toward your chest, pressing your forearms down. Draw the other knee to your chest, engaging your abdominals and pressing your forearms down as you lift your shoulders.
- Slowly slide your heels up the wall, bringing your legs together as one.
- Once you're upside down, press down again into your forearms, lift your shoulders and engage your abdominals as you reach up through your heels.
- You can actually do this pose with very little weight on the head to maintain space in your cervical spine (neck).
- Stay here for ten to fifty breaths, focusing on the movement of energy up and down the entire length of the body. Allow gravity to draw energy to the crown of the head.
- When you're ready to come out of the pose, bend your knees slowly. Press your forearms down vigorously as you lift your shoulders. Slowly release your toes to the floor and rest in Child's Pose again.

Savasana: Corpse Pose: This pose is the ultimate surrender to the divine. When we actually die, our bodies will remain as our souls travel on to the next phase of our adventure. When this happens, we'll truly understand that the body is only a temporary home for the eternal soul. Ram Dass says all of life is preparation for death. When we die, we become so expansive and so connected that we must spend our time down here preparing for the grandness of it.

Guided Relaxation for Merging with the Divine

You can do this guided relaxation while in Savasana. You may want to download the recording from www.e-yoga.com or have someone read it to you.

Lying on your back, separate your feet to outer hip distance. Turn your palms up and place your arms a few inches from your sides. If your lower back hurts, roll up a blanket and place it under your knees. You may also want to place a blanket under your head so it doesn't roll to one side.

Take a few moments to follow the breath moving in and out of your body. The breath is the vehicle for *prana*. You are consciousness observing the movement of the vital life force in and out of the body. Let go of your attachment to the body as me or mine. Allow the body to be part of the vital energy, not separate from it. Allow the body to be part of creation. You do not own the body. The body is a vehicle made for you by your creator to travel through this lifetime. When the time comes for you to expand out of this body, you will no longer need it. Practice letting it go. *Pause.*

Relax the muscles away from the bones. Let the bones settle into the earth. Allow the skin to soften and become less of a barrier, more porous, so that it mixes with the space around it. Feel your consciousness expand as the body diminishes. *Pause.*

Let the body drop away. Allow your consciousness to expand. Merge with the floor, the walls, the ceiling, the air in the room. Merge with the space outside the room. Continue to grow in your consciousness, larger and larger and larger, until you experience yourself as the planets, the stars, the cosmos. *Pause.*

There is nowhere you need to go, nothing you need to do or prove. You are one with the consciousness of the universe. You are one with the divine. You and the divine are one. There are no more questions. There are no more answers. There's no more striving. There is only the deepest, most pervasive sense of equanimity—peace that passes understanding. Perfect peace. *Pause.*

Rest in this perfect peace. See that all that happens in the physical world is simply a dance of energy and form, light and dark, Shiva and Shakti. You are the still point of consciousness at the center of it all. Undying, unchanging, formless and eternal.

Long pause.

Note that as you choose to reconnect your consciousness to the form of the body, you now know this is a choice. You no longer feel that the body and the mind are all of who you are. You now know that you are everything and no "thing". You have experienced the ultimate surrender. You have reunited with the one who created your consciousness and your body. Rest in this sweet knowing for as long as you like.

Long pause.

Begin to gently draw your consciousness back into the body. Notice the breath moving in and out. In and out. In and out. Feel the back of the body resting on the floor. Feel the skin on your face. Begin to move your fingers and toes. Gently stretch your arms overhead. Draw your knees into the body. Roll over to your right side and rest here for a while. When you're ready, you can sit up and take a few moments to listen to the sounds in the room and reacquaint with the physical plane. When you're ready to move, take care to become fully aware in your body before you get up.

Remembering, Forgetting, Remembering Again

Once we come home to a dark house, unlock the door, turn on the light and—"Surprise!"—discover that we're one with the creator of the universe, this doesn't mean that we'll never again forget. We won't always be in bliss as we stand in line for an hour with our child at an amusement park only to discover that he or she is still too small to ride the ride. We may forget when our boss belittles us in front of our co-workers that this is only the boss of our job and not of our soul. We may forget, when our significant other doesn't seem to understand or even care how we're feeling, that it's only on the most superficial surface that we're in conflict. We may forget that underneath all the small things that cause us to suffer, there's one big thing, bigger than anything we can fathom, holding it all, allowing it to unfold and evolve in the beautiful dance of life.

When we want to connect to this grandness all we ever need to do is ask. When we want to experience it for ourselves, all we have to do is sit still, quiet down and let go. Easier said than done, but absolutely possible. As the Buddha said, "If it were not possible for you to be free from suffering, I would not be teaching you how."

CHAPTER 9

Putting It All Together

"We are all just walking each other home."
— Ram Dass

I showed up broken for my first day of Yoga Teacher Training, arriving two weeks late because my spine was so severely misaligned I couldn't fly. My body was overweight, my skin broken out and my mind foggy from the two weeks of heavy drinking and drugs that preceded my bon voyage. I fumbled through a Mysore-style Ashtanga yoga practice, watching the people around me for clues as to what we were supposed to be doing, and when it was finally over I passed out on my little blue mat.

The sound of a new teacher's voice woke me—our Iyengar yoga teacher. He told us that this nine months would transform us on every level: mind, body and spirit. I was twenty-two and I thought he was full of shit. *I've already transformed*, I said to myself, thinking back to my six weeks in India and three months at the Yoga ashram in San Francisco. Little did I know, that year of soul searching had been only the beginning of this epic journey.

My nine months in yoga teacher training was a gestation period for my soul. From conception—the moment I arrived, dragging my exhausted body home every morning after a three-hour practice so I could eat like a horse and sleep like the dead before going back for more in the afternoon—through the uncertainty of the second trimester—realizing there was so much I didn't know and trying to understand it all—to the last trimester—blissing out in my strong, light body and glowing skin, surrounded by people who had once been strangers but were now and forever family, the experience challenged me on all levels, and as my teacher foreshadowed, it transformed me, too.

But I was also right, because still, at my essence, I am the same being I was before it started. I am the same soul I was before this birth and the same one I will be in the next lifetime and the next. The difference is, after completing the training, I had so many more tools for working with the challenges that life continually offers.

Doing the work of transformation doesn't give you a pass from the trials and tribulations of life. It does help you move through them with so much more grace, balance and ease.

Transformation shows you that you're stronger than you thought you were. You have the capacity to do more than you ever thought possible. It reminds you that you have unique gifts that the world needs. As one of my teachers says, I will continue to practice until all beings experience samsara as nirvana. Samsara are the deep grooves in the mind that cause us to suffer. Nirvana is the state of bliss, in which we truly experience everything that's happening as perfect.

Pema Chodron writes in her book *Practicing Peace in Times of War*, "When you open yourself to the continually changing, impermanent, dynamic nature of your own being and of reality, you increase your capacity to love and care about other people and your capacity to not be afraid. You're able to keep your eyes open, your heart open, and your mind open. And you notice when you get caught up in prejudice, bias, and aggression. You develop an enthusiasm for no longer watering those negative seeds, from now until the day you die. And, you begin to think of your life as offering endless opportunities to start to do things differently."

It's true. We receive endless opportunities to do things differently. Through this work we begin to develop enthusiasm not only for no longer watering the seeds of negativity but also for planting and watering the seeds of our potential. The word *potential* contains the word *potent*, which means powerful, something that's chock-full of the ingredients needed to make change.

We are potent beings, full of potential. When we water the seeds of our potential, they grow in ways that we never could have predicted. As I've mentioned, a student who first came to class as an embittered police officer with post-traumatic stress after 9/11 decided to begin watering the seeds of his potential through many of the practices in this book, especially yoga and meditation. By trusting in the process and in himself, he was able to transform into something completely different, a yoga teacher, someone who helps other people inhabit their bodies and quiet their minds.

We all have the potential to create our lives anew. It's never too late. You're never too far gone. The transformative power of the universe is always available to you.

Honoring Our Transformation

When I think of the process of transformation, Caitlyn Jenner comes to mind. Being one of the world's greatest athletes married to a famous woman with several gorgeous children wasn't enough, because in that body and that role, she wasn't able to experience and express her true authenticity.

Although it must have been terrifying to share her truth with her family and then with the world, eventually she had no other choice. Just like the caterpillar has no choice but to enter the cocoon and liquefy in order to emerge as the beautiful butterfly. We as humans may try to hide out and act like everything is fine just as it is, but in our hearts we know there's always more for us out there. We're never done exploring.

As T. S. Eliot wrote in his poem "Little Gidding":
> We shall not cease from exploration
> And the end of all our exploring
> Will be to arrive where we started
> And know the place for the first time.

After a particularly big shift for one of my clients, he confessed that he liked the old him better. When we dug a little deeper, he realized that what he meant was that the old him was more comfortable. He knew that guy really well. He knew what to expect, even though some of it wasn't good. We talked about how, even when we try to remain the same, it isn't possible. The world is a place of continual change. But I reminded him that at his essence he *is* the same being he has always been and always will be. I encouraged him to remember how he felt as a child, how he feels as a middle-aged man and how he might feel as an old man during those moments when he's happy and content. "This part of you will never change," I told him. "This is who you really are."

That's what we're doing when we're transforming. We aren't really trying to change into someone else. Like Caitlyn Jenner, we're all just trying to step into the most authentic version of ourselves. Then, if we're brave, we stand in the light so others can be the witness to our true selves.

Deepening Our Transformation

You may be wondering how you can continue to deepen your transformation. Whenever I come back from a retreat, I feel the glow of inner work for a few weeks, and then inevitably the grit of everyday life creeps back in. This is not a bad thing. This is where the rubber meets the road. This is when we have the chance to dip into our new tool kits and use those tools that help us move through the rough spots with greater ease.

When you finish this book, I encourage you to go back through it and mark the exercises that were particularly helpful for you, though I don't imagine you'll do every one of them on a daily or weekly basis. If you're like me, you might set very high expectations for yourself. Remember, this isn't a race. This is your life unfolding. You don't have to go at anyone's pace other than your own. You can think of the exercises in this book like spices on a spice rack. Which spice will bring the best flavor to what you're currently working through? Coriander doesn't go well in banana bread, but cumin is fabulous in chili. Once you familiarize yourself with the different flavors of the teachings, you'll be able to pull the perfect one from the shelf when you need it. And once you've completed this journey, many of these practices and teachings will spontaneously pop into your mind when you need them.

One of my clients came to every single session hungover for more than a year. She used to hide her face behind her hair and keep her feelings bottled up inside. Through yoga, meditation, shamanic healing and the 12-step program, she has made a profound transformation. She recently sent me a text saying she'd been asked to speak to heroin addicts at a detox clinic. She was supposed to tell them her story of being deeply mired in alcohol and drug addiction and then finding her way to sobriety. She was terrified that she wouldn't know what to say or that she wouldn't say the right thing. I encouraged her to remember that all she had to do was show up and tell the truth.

As scared as she was, that's what she did. When she finished, she sent me another text saying that, second only to getting sober, talking to this group of people who were in the hopeless place she had once been was probably the best thing she'd ever done. Amen! If this isn't grace, I don't know what is.

Another thing we must remember is that we aren't doing this work alone. Whether you believe in a higher power or not, there are beings of light surrounding each one of us. They show up as a friend sending a text saying, "I was just thinking of you and wondering how you are doing." When this happens, tell the truth. If you aren't well, let them know and be willing to ask for support.

Early in our work together, this same woman came to me for a healing session in which she experienced some powerful shifts. Two hours later, I saw her on the street completely hammered. We were surprised to see each other, but I don't think it was a coincidence. I think her angels and my angels got together and decided to offer her a nudge toward her destiny.

One of the things she often tells me is that I saw in her what she couldn't see in herself. My husband has continually seen the goodness in me when I can't see it in myself. This is one of the things I find so incredible about him. Remember to see your own goodness, your own potential, and when you can't, surround yourself with people who can. If you're surrounded by people who are stuck and have no desire to move forward, it may be time to invest in some new friendships. This isn't to say you can't love your old friends, but as my mother always told me, we are who we spend time with. As humans, we can't help but become like the people we're around all the time. I see this in my son when he's frustrated and starts talking to me the way I talk to him when I'm frustrated. He also has an amazing ability to speak in an American accent to me and then turn to his Australian father and say the same phrase to him with an Aussie accent. This demonstrates the power of the voices we hear on a daily basis.

Another way we can deepen our transformation is by being of service to others. This doesn't mean you have to go door-to-door preaching the gospel of whatever has worked for you. You can if you want, but who has the time? It means that if a blind person is struggling to walk across the street in traffic, you take the time to walk with her. You remember that we're all blinded sometimes and need a little guidance. It means that when a homeless person asks you for money, you don't ignore them or shove the money into the cup without looking. You pause. You see them as just like you in a different situation and you breathe in the reality of your shared humanness. You take that extra minute to chat with an elderly person on your street, to let them ooh and ahh over your baby. You ask if they need help with anything. You don't have to go to a war-torn country to help, although you certainly can. There are endless opportunities to be of service to those in need right where you are now. And every time you serve, you grow stronger in your own transformation.

There's a man who sits in his electric wheelchair by the stairs to the subway asking for money. I used to stick a dollar into his cup once or twice a week before hastily moving on. But one day my higher power nudged me to stop and talk to him. I told him my name and asked his. He can't speak, but he has a small keyboard on his computer. It took his wild fingers a long time to land on one key and well over a minute for him to type his name, Mario. It's amazing how learning someone's name can create an instant deep connection. While I may be helping him out with a little money, he helps me even more by reminding me to slow down and share human moments with another being. If we see service not as trying to save everyone but as being part of the flow of energy moving toward the greater good, there's no *me* helping *you*. There's only life helping life unfold.

Every year one of my clients invites my husband and I to a charity gala for a homeless shelter in New York City. At the beginning of the meal, a video depicts one of the residents who has transformed his or her life through the help of this organization. The last video I saw focused on a woman who had been on her own since she was a teenager, had been a drug addict, a drug dealer and a sex worker and found salvation through this organization. Several years later, not only was she clean and sober, but she had become a certified drug and alcohol counselor and persuaded her husband to seek help through the programs offered through the organization. She now counsels other women who are working to recover from addiction and reclaim their lives. Can you imagine if even one of the women she works with does the same thing? The circle of service will continue to ripple out and out and out until we all experience Samsara as Nirvana.

The poet Rilke wrote, "I live my life in widening circles that reach out across the world. I may not complete this last one, but I give myself to it." This is what we do. We give ourselves to it fully. We make ourselves the offering to this beautiful life. We risk being full participants in the unfolding.

Help from Our Friends

As we continue on the path of transformation, we may find we need more support. As a lifelong seeker, I've always found support and solace in books, but nothing quite compares to the sound of a supportive voice or being in the same room with someone who's there to help guide you on your journey.

I teach group yoga classes on a weekly basis, and I'm sometimes surprised to see the same people coming back again and again. I think to myself, *I'm not sure if I have anything more to offer them.* But then I think of my favorite restaurant and how I can order the same meal every week for a year and have a new and nourishing experience each time.

As I was adding my final edits of this book at my mother's home, an old friend of hers, whom she's shared more than forty years with, came over for dinner. After we put the kids to bed, we shared the ways our higher power has been working mysteriously in our lives. I shared an excerpt from this book, and they both cried and then offered their own spiritual growth experiences. By the end we were laughing through our tears, which in my opinion is one of the best emotions available. When we gather together and talk about the everyday miracles in our lives and the ways we've been supported as we move through the challenges of life, it make the journey a little easier. It reminds us that we are not alone.

Just after graduating college I booked myself in for a weekend Ashtanga yoga retreat, but the night before the retreat I went to a bar in San Francisco by myself, met a couple of funny guys who were headed to a wedding in Sonoma and decided to go with them instead. We had a blast, but it was fleeting. It took me a few more months to start realizing that while life is made up of moments, we need to cultivate some kind of grounding, some kind of mindfulness to enjoy them, and we need to adhere to some kind of code in order to live in a way that doesn't cause harm. When we're ready, we answer the call. Until then, we do other things.

Don't be too hard on yourself. The creator of the universe will never stop pursuing you. You haven't missed your surprise party. One day, when you least expect it, you'll open the door and be floored by the perfection that is you standing there ready to meet you.

In Closing

This book is a culmination of nearly two decades of exploration through travel, learning, teaching, writing and healing. I began writing the book just after discovering I was pregnant with my second child. As my beloved editor parceled out the tasks that would make the process of writing so much more accessible, I dragged myself to the computer to complete each one, combating nausea and exhaustion at the same time. She encouraged me to just do what I could, a little bit each day.

I experienced an upswing during the second trimester, when my energy was high and my belly manageable. During the third trimester, everything I had hurt. I could barely write because my wrists were so swollen and my hands went numb after ten or fifteen minutes on the keyboard. And after the baby was born, I went into a kind of sleep-deprived, waking dream state that I continue to muddle through.

The night before completing this chapter, we started sleep-training our daughter. I was blessed with healthy adorable children but not naturally good sleepers. After an hour and a half of shuteye in the crib that was once her brother's, she bolted awake and began to wail. For an hour I tried everything short of feeding her to get her to go back to sleep. She wasn't having any of it.

We'd had to start sleep-training our son at eleven months after, in a sleep-deprived state, I thought jumping off the subway stairs to catch a train in flat dress shoes was a good idea. I made the train, but I broke both my feet. Three years later, he lay in his little bed beside his sister's crib, sleeping soundly, oblivious to the howling. This gave me hope that even though it hurt so much to listen to her cry, I was doing the right thing. She, too, would soon be a sleeper.

When he finally woke up during her third round of screaming, he asked his daddy if she was okay.

"Yes, bud," Daddy said. "She's just learning how to sleep. She has to figure out how to soothe herself instead of waiting for Mommy and Daddy to do it."

"Oh," he said and turned over to go back to sleep.

We're all in some stage of the sleep-training process, learning how to wake up, soothe ourselves and then rest in the perfection of what is. At 5 a.m. I lay in bed praying that my daughter would learn quickly so she didn't have to suffer too much, and I have to admit I became a teensy bit demanding with the big mama upstairs. Then, after a particularly aggressive prayer, my daughter went quiet suddenly and stayed asleep for three more hours. I was embarrassed, the way you are when you take out your frustrations on a customer-service agent who's helpful and gracious. "Oh, thanks. Sorry about the attitude. Things are a little tense around here."

I thought for sure that when she woke up at eight, she'd be sulking, turning away from me as she remembered how I hung her out to dry, but she looked up at me with her big, tired blue eyes, serious for a moment and then all smiles.

I write these last few words standing at the kitchen counter with her strapped to my chest, refuting any doubts I might have had about the truth that we're all one. May we all be like this precious baby during our own transformations—trusting in those who are here to support us, willing to try to do the work on our own, vulnerable enough in the process to express our fears and feelings. May we forgive those who have hurt us, because they might be our greatest teachers. And most important, may we always remember to smile.

Namaste,
EJ

---

[i] "WJS Article, Nov 2014

About the Author

Since 2001, **Elizabeth Flint** has taught yoga and meditation to tens of thousands of people, leading workshops, retreats and teacher trainings in New York City and around the globe. She weaves shamanic healing and coaching into her work, creating a powerful method of supporting people as they transform their lives. Elizabeth is a former Pulliam Fellowship recipient. Her blog, Namaste, EJ, has been featured in Yoga Journal, Yoga City NYC and the syndicated column "Among Friends." She lives with her family just outside the bustle of New York City.

Printed in the United States
By Bookmasters